A Trainer's Guide to
Web-Based Instruction

AMERICAN SOCIETY FOR TRAINING & DEVELOPMENT

Learning Technologies

A Trainer's Guide to Web-Based Instruction

Getting Started on Intranet- and Internet-Based Training

Jay Alden

ASTD

Ordering information: Books published by the American Society for Training & Development can be ordered by calling 800.628.2783.

Library of Congress Catalog Card Number: 98-70594
ISBN: 1-56286-084-4

Editor's note: We have done our level best to provide accurate URL addresses in this book. However, due to the ever-changing nature of the Web, some of these addresses may change.

Table of Contents

About the Learning Technologies Series

For centuries, the technology for transferring skills and knowledge changed little—one human being taught others. Generations of classroom trainers deployed this time-honored "chalk and talk" approach. Only the advent of the film, the filmstrip, video, and the slide, and overhead projectors marred an education and training landscape otherwise devoid of technological innovation. All of this, however, is currently undergoing rapid change—the snail-paced rate of innovation appears ready to give way to a torrent of change as new technologies create the possibility of more effective and efficient learning.

Increasingly, the transfer of information, knowledge, and skills can be facilitated by a variety of electronic media, often reducing the need for time-intensive transfer based on the interaction of human beings. This represents both a challenge and opportunity for those professionals who specialize in workplace learning and performance.[1]

A Trainer's Guide to Web-Based Instruction: Getting Started on Intranet- and Internet-Based Training is the first book in a planned series of short, easily understood learning technologies books that will give these same professionals the tools to become part of this exciting technology revolution. Other books in this series will provide detailed step-by-step instructions on how to design and deliver Web-based instruction, while still others in the series may examine how to evaluate the effectiveness of Web-based training.

In addition to providing valuable information, these books will strive toward a consistent use of terminology to help standardize an increasingly confusing lexicon of terms. (See the Glossary for more on definitions associated with learning technologies.)

We hope this series of books will enable all learning and performance professionals to effectively use these powerful new tools.

---

[1] From November 1997 *Training & Development* magazine article, "Trends That Affect Learning and Performance Improvement" by ASTD Research staff: Laurie J. Bassi, Scott Cheney, and Mark Van Buren.

Preface

I have personally been involved with training technology since the early "behavioral" days of programmed instruction (B.F. Skinner's "frames," Norman Crowder's "branches," and Tom Gilbert's "operant spans") and even tried my hand at a mechanically based teaching machine. I got it working for about a 15-minute stint one time and then left it to rust. I jumped in with both feet when computer-assisted instruction emerged from the murky world of business computers. My first computer-based training program was written in the Basic language and ran from an eight-inch floppy disk on a Xerox personal computer. (This was just before IBM came out with its first PC.) Then, Xerox went back to making copiers and I went back to the classroom—for a while anyway.

I was also a reasonably early adopter of online instruction. The institution where I work tried its hand at a completely online course in 1993. We recruited 40 people to participate in an experimental training program. Half of them were randomly assigned to an online course and the other half to a traditional classroom version of the same course. Everyone who began the classroom course finished it and gave glowing reviews. We brought the online students to the school one day and showed them how to use the software. (Remember, in 1993, they had to learn a number of computer commands just to read and send messages.) Off they went to learn from their homes and offices. Five of these students eventually logged on. One of them even logged on twice, but that was it. It took another three years for us to get up the nerve to try it again.

What I learned from these experiences is pretty obvious—technology is not enough. I am certainly not alone in quickly embracing new technologies and applying them to instructional situations. Too often we all become enamored with the technological capabilities of our bright and shiny devices and ignore fundamental learning theory. We probably spent much too much time working through the novelty of programmed instruction, teaching machines, and computer-based instruction to get to the point where they worked well.

Now look at the fearsome power of the World Wide Web as presented in this book. It can present information visually, aurally, and dynamically in untold numbers of colors and sounds. Students have almost instant access to a world of informational resources from the absurd to the divine. They can communicate with the instructor, with each other, and with experts in the field no matter where they are located or what time they choose to be available. They can enter a virtual three-dimensional world that is realistic, abstract, or fantasy and look around to see what's there or how it works. They can fly a spaceship even if they can't drive a car. Students can work together as a team on a common project even if they have never met, don't speak the same language, or are located in three different time zones. What can't be done on the World Wide Web? Not much! Just use your imagination. Yet, we still risk the danger of emphasizing capability over functionality.

The purpose of this book is to explore the power of the World Wide Web for training and education. Yes, it will describe the wondrous capabilities of the Web, but we hope they are well grounded in the functions of learning and instruction. We don't want to use a capability just because we can. We use it because it advances our ability to help our students learn while either making training conveniently available or reducing expenses associated with classroom instruction. Don't let the bells, whistles, and glitz of the Web make us blind to effective instructional practice. Many of the capabilities of the World Wide Web can be applied appropriately to training and education without a major investment. The communications infrastructure of most modern organizations provides all the technology you need—a Web presence, e-mail, newsgroups, and so forth—to gain astonishing learning functionality. Again, keep your eye on the real target—greater learning, enhanced availability, reduced training-related expenses, or all three.

An equal, but opposite, pitfall of Web-based instruction is to focus on just those capabilities that allow you to mimic the best of classroom instruction. We can use the multimedia capabilities of the Web to emulate an in-depth lecture by the instructor. We can use e-mail both ways so the instructor and students can ask and answer questions of each other, just as they do in class. We can use conferencing capabilities to divide students into small groups and have them work together on a common response to a project or a case study, which they present to the entire class. If all we do is imitate a traditional classroom, then Web-based instruction will be a second-rate reproduction of the classroom experience. Those extraordinary capabilities of the World Wide Web permit us to apply learning theory in ways that are inconceivable in the classroom. As you proceed through this book considering the instructional capabilities of the Web, continue using your imagination, but link those capabilities to meaningful learning functionality. The technological capabilities will change rapidly, but instructional functionality will remain stable.

The functionality we looked to build into programmed instruction, teaching machines, and computer-based instruction thrives today on the World Wide Web.

Chapter 1. Teaching and Learning Online

Web-Based Instruction: What It Is and Isn't

Web-based instruction is a fairly recent development that is also known by a number of other labels—*Online Instruction, Web-Based Training (WBT), Learning Over the Internet/intranet*—just to name a few. Simply stated, Web-based instruction is the use of intranets or the Internet to conduct courses of instruction. It is one form of *distance learning.*

Let's start with a formal definition. According to the American Council on Education, distance learning is…

> "a system and a process that connects learners with distributed learning resources. While distance learning takes a wide variety of forms, all distance learning is characterized by: (1) separation of place and/or time between instructor and learner, among learners, and/or between learners and learning resources, and (2) interaction between the learner and the instructor, among learners, and/or between learners and learning resources conducted through one or more media; use of electronic media is not necessarily required." (American Council on Education, *Guiding Principles for Distance Education in a Learning Society,* 1996, p. 10.)

This definition certainly includes Web-based instruction because instructors, students, and resources are separated from one another, and communication networks and computers are the media that provide interaction among all those people and resources. The definition would also include the use of other electronic media such as telephones and video satellite networks.

Three Primary Modes Used for Distance Learning

1. Remote Classroom (Interactive Television or ITV)

Instruction is delivered to clusters of students who meet in a classroom environment physically separated from the centralized school or institution. Instructions may be delivered simultaneously to one or more remote classrooms. A staff coordinator or facilitator may or may not be present at each

remote site. Information is presented to the student group from the central "school," usually through some form of video interface that includes the ability to display graphic images. Comments and questions by students in the remote classrooms are transmitted back to the instructor in the central school by telephone or an audiovisual system. After class, students can communicate individually with the instructor by telephone or e-mail.

2. Virtual Classroom (Synchronous Online Instruction)

Instruction is delivered to individual students working on personal computers at their homes or offices. All the students are connected to the network at the same time. The instructor has complete control over what the students see and hear on their computers. The instructor can control slide presentations, video clips, live speech, a *whiteboard* display, or even special software applications displayed on the students' computers. The instructor can ask questions that all students can answer at the same time using their keyboard or by mouse click. The instructor can view the answers of each student and of the group. Students can raise their hands electronically to ask a question or make a comment. The instructor can even pass control to an individual student who can comment orally, add to the common whiteboard display, or present a visual that all other students can view. This approach emulates a classroom environment, and the class is run electronically in real time as if everyone were in the same room.

3. Anytime Classroom (Asynchronous Online Instruction)

Instruction is delivered to individual students working on personal computers at their homes or offices. The information may be conveyed to their computers via telecommunications or by a CD-ROM sent through the mail.

Practical Tips

Key Factors to Consider Before Moving to Web-Based Instruction

Web-based training makes sense if the following situations exist:
- Costs are high using traditional training methods.
- Some key students can't make it to the classroom.
- Access to an intranet/Internet exists and support is available.
- The program's content and activities are appropriate for the Web.
- Participating students really want to complete the training.
- Course content must be updated frequently.

The students tend to work through the materials independently, setting their own schedules and pace of instruction. The students interact with the instructor and other students using one form or another of telecommunications. They typically do this with asynchronous means such as *e-mail, voice mail, listservs,* and *computer conferencing,* and sometimes with synchronous methods such as *chats, videoconferencing,* and *telephone conferences.*

In some cases, the students can also interact with programmed questions and activities embedded in the course materials and receive feedback without the intervention of an instructor.

Anytime classroom is the most common approach to Web-based instruction. Most of the communications involved in this form of distance learning are conducted over the World Wide Web of the Internet, or over an organization's intranet—which is a kind of small-scale Internet with very limited access. This book will concentrate primarily on this mode of distance learning.

The *virtual classroom* mode of distance learning can also be considered a form of Web-based instruction because although most versions now run on special voice or data networks, this approach can be conducted over the Web. This book will occasionally touch on this mode of distance learning. The *remote classroom* mode of distance learning is almost never run over the Web, so it will not be viewed as a form of Web-based instruction and will not be dealt with in this book.

Why Organizations Use Web-Based Instruction

Here are some of the many reasons why an organization may use Web-based instruction for some or all of its training programs.

To Reduce Travel Expenses
With Web-based instruction, students can complete courses from their desktop computers at home or at work. They can even work on training courses using their notebook computers when they're on the road. The point is that they do not have to travel to a central classroom and they don't incur costs for transportation, hotels, or meals. If a training program involves high travel-related expenses, the payoff in Web-based instruction could be substantial.

For Outreach to Other Students
Frequently, some students just can't get away to attend training. Travel time and expenses may be prohibitive, and even if the training is conducted in the same town or even the same building, they might be too busy to spend two, three, or more days in a classroom. They may have a major

scheduling conflict with their job at some point during the training. With Web-based instruction, the institution can reach students like these who otherwise would not attend the training.

To Improve Training Quality

Web-based instruction has many features that would be difficult to duplicate in many classrooms. For example, online students must be active; they can't just sit back and passively listen to the instructor. They can learn at their own pace and in their own style. They can interrupt the instruction whenever they wish, and reach out to the enormous wealth of information and educational resources available on the Web. They can produce products and participate in projects on the computer, individually or with others. They can share these products or projects with other students or the instructor at the push of a button and receive individualized feedback. Some organizations embark on Web-based instruction not just because of the added convenience or economic benefits, but because they feel they will get better results.

To Improve Training Efficiency or Timing

For the same reasons that Web-based instruction can increase the quality of training, it can also reduce the time necessary to reach a specified level of performance. Research has demonstrated that computer-based instruction using active, self-paced learning with individualized feedback has often reduced total training time by 30 or 40 percent. Since Web-based instruction shares many of the attributes of computer-based learning, it would be no surprise to achieve similar time reductions when training is delivered online.

Another advantage is that when the training is updated, materials can be revised at just one location and the new version becomes instantly available. Moreover, Web-based instruction can be scheduled on a "just-in-time" basis, exactly when the people on the job need it most.

To Boost the Image of the Training Organization

Although it is never stated openly, some organizations introduce Web-based training programs because it says, "We are with it, we are high technology, we are a 21st century organization." Some might argue the business merits of this strategy, but it can be a valuable tactic.

For example, suppose a training organization is struggling for survival. If introducing Web-based instruction would improve its image and at the same time enable it to reduce travel expenses associated with training, reach out to new students, or improve training quality or efficiency, it could serve both the business and the political interests of the organization.

Differences Between Web-Based and Classroom Courses

There are some clear-cut differences between classroom courses and comparable courses conducted online and some differences that are not so obvious. Review the 10 instructional characteristics listed in table 1 and

	Table 1. Differences between Web-based and classroom instruction.						
Characteristics	**Much More for Classroom** Courses		Roughly the **Same**			**Much More for Web-Based** Courses	
A. Time and effort to develop instructional materials	①	②	③	④	⑤	⑥	⑦
B. Time and effort to update instructional materials	①	②	③	④	⑤	⑥	⑦
C. Amount of calendar time for students to complete course	①	②	③	④	⑤	⑥	⑦
D. Student access to and competence with computer systems	①	②	③	④	⑤	⑥	⑦
E. Administrative costs associated with course	①	②	③	④	⑤	⑥	⑦
F. Ability to apply multi-media materials	①	②	③	④	⑤	⑥	⑦
G. Extent of information resources available to learners	①	②	③	④	⑤	⑥	⑦
H. Amount of interactive activity required of students	①	②	③	④	⑤	⑥	⑦
I. Amount of learning resulting from course	①	②	③	④	⑤	⑥	⑦
J. Ability to evaluate student learning	①	②	③	④	⑤	⑥	⑦

indicate the extent to which you believe they typically differ between classroom and Web-based courses. Then, check your responses against the author's ratings that follow the table.

Here are my responses to the above comparisons between Web-based and classroom instruction, based on many years of experience using both methods:

A. Time and Effort to Develop Instructional Materials: 5 to 6

It does take more time and effort to develop Web-based instruction. Generally, Web-based materials have to go through an additional step to translate them into the languages of the Web (HTML, GIF, JAVA and others that will be explained in chapter two). This difference is diminishing, however, because push-button translation of this type is being included in progressively more standard word processing, graphics, and authoring software packages.

B. Time and Effort to Update: 2 to 3

Web-based instructional materials are easier to locate and revise because they are already converted to electronic form and stored in a central repository. Even more important, revised Web-based materials can be automatically and instantaneously distributed to students. Whenever students connect to the Web server, they have immediate access to the latest edition of course materials.

C. Calendar Time to Complete Course: 3 to 7

(Highly dependent upon scheduling models.) Experience indicates that asynchronous individual desktop courses take about 30 times as long as classroom courses. That is, a classroom training course conducted in three consecutive days will require about 90 days to finish, if it is conducted over the Web and students can connect to the course when they wish, and if asynchronous conferencing among students and the instructor is required. If the classroom version of the course is scheduled using a university model, with one or two meetings per week for a few hours each, then both approaches would take about the same amount of time. If the Web-based version of the course used a purely synchronous strategy like the virtual classroom model, the required calendar time would be similar to that of a classroom course. If the interaction in the Web-based course was limited to instructional programming built into the materials—with no discussion among students or with the instructor—then the online course might take even less calendar time to complete than a corresponding classroom course.

D. Computer Access and Competence: 6 to 7

There is not much controversy on this item. Web-based instruction can work only if the students have easy access to computer hardware and are comfortable using it. While it is true that systems are becoming more readily available and easier to use, computers are still not widely enough available to make widespread Web-based instruction the rule. For at least the next few years, this will continue to be a serious limitation on Web-based instruction. Training organizations and educational institutions thinking about introducing Web-based instruction for members of the general population should also plan to build an effective technical support capability for students.

E. Administrative Costs: 3 to 5

These costs depend on which items you include. If extensive travel is necessary for classroom instruction and if you factor in the cost of the classroom facilities, Web-based instruction is probably a wonderful bargain. On the other hand, if existing classroom facilities will remain even if all courses are converted to Web-based instruction and if your organization provides computers to students, it will cost much more to train using the Web. In most cases, reducing costs in some areas roughly balances additional costs in others.

F. Ability to Apply Multimedia: 2 to 3

Multimedia techniques such as music, sounds, 3D graphics, animation, and video can be used in both classroom and Web-based courses. Right now, it is still easier to use them in the classroom. A classroom instructor can usually project full-screen images from video recorders, CD players, and computer systems without problems or delays. Unfortunately, this is not true for the Web. A great deal of time is often required to download multimedia segments from the Web, and this can be distracting to the student. Techniques are being developed to help expedite this process and make it less painful, but they are not quite here yet.

G. Availability of Information Resources: 5 to 6

Here is where Web-based instruction really shines. While extensive learning resources including videotapes, live demonstrations, guest speakers, and experts can be brought in to add to the dynamic environment of a classroom, the resources available to students over the Web are breathtaking. Students can access and search through the library holdings of a thousand universities; they can use e-mail to contact and interview world-class authorities or the actual participants in a case study; they can participate in other online courses on specialized topics associated with your course.

Indeed, there may be *too much* information available on the Web, and that may be a problem.

H. Required Student Activity: 5 to 7

Online students must be active; they can't just sit back and passively listen to the instructor. At the very least, they must click on the "Next" button for the next bit of information. Web-based courses often require students to answer questions individually by clicking on possible alternatives or entering short answers into a form. They can engage in personal conversations via e-mail with the instructor or other students. They are often required to participate in or even initiate online asynchronous conferences. In some Web-based courses, students collaborate on projects using a shared work space on the screen (a whiteboard) or take part in synchronous online chats with other students. They can be immersed in a virtual world walking through a city, or a human body, or a motor, or participate in a realistic simulation flying a helicopter or operating on a patient. In contrast to a classroom, nothing happens in a Web-based course unless every student takes some kind of action.

I. Amount of Learning: 4 to 5

This factor is somewhat linked to student activity, above. The more active students are, the more they learn. We should expect a high level of learning to the extent that a Web-based course requires and stimulates a great deal of activity by the students. Because interaction is more likely a part of Web-based instruction than it is for classroom instruction, we should expect a higher level of learning. However, many factors can influence learning and some of them—for example, a student's learning style—might favor the face-to-face nature of classroom teaching. To date, most research seems to demonstrate that there are no significant differences between the amount of learning in classroom and distance learning courses.

J. Ability to Evaluate Learning: 5 to 6

This factor is also connected to student activity. When the student takes action on the computer, that action is recorded, stored, and made available for evaluation and grading. This makes it easy to measure a student's progress with Web-based tests, collaborative group work, papers and other projects, and participation in simulations. The difficulty is choosing which activities to evaluate.

Situations in Which Web-Based Instruction Makes Sense

From a Business Perspective

To sum up, here are the situations in which you should consider using Web-based instruction from a business perspective:

● if the organization has high expenses associated with the travel, lodging and meals of people attending training programs

● if many of your prospective students find it difficult to break away from their work and attend a face-to-face training program

● if you and your students have relatively easy access to desktop or laptop computers that can be connected to your intranet or the Web, and you all are reasonably competent in using these systems (or you can build a technical support service to help users install and operate specialized software).

From an Instructional Perspective

Here are the situations in which you should consider using Web-based courses, from an instructional perspective:

● if the critical content of the course can be easily conveyed by words, pictures, and extensive discussion between the instructor and students

● if there are adequate incentives or the students are highly motivated to complete the training, even though the course might require an extended period of time and they—the students—will bear the primary burden to initiate many of the actions in their learning and development

● if the information provided by the training tends to change rapidly and often, or it is difficult to predict and schedule exactly when the students will need that information.

Chapter 2. Presentation of Information

Multimedia Capabilities of the Web

A large part of an effective training course involves the presentation of information. The Web offers a rich environment for presenting information in many ways that can be used to make an online course not only effective, but engaging, enjoyable, and interesting.

Ways of Presenting Information

Text

Obviously, the Web can present information in the form of text. A Web page is created using a special language called the Hypertext Markup Language (HTML). As in word processing, a page designer using HTML can change the face, size, boldness, color, and style of the font, and can underline selected words and phrases. However, it usually doesn't pay to use very fancy fonts, because they won't show up on users' screens unless they have those fonts available on their systems. The textual information can be presented in any language unless the language requires special symbols that are not supported by the user's system.

If it is absolutely necessary to use a variety of unusual fonts, the designer can avoid this problem by introducing those fonts using *graphic type*. In this technique, the textual information is actually inserted into the Web page as a graphic, which can be read by all users' systems rather than as a type font. Incidentally, some old forms of browsers can view only textual information, so it may be wise to let students know that they will need a certain generation of browser to participate in the course.

Simple Graphics

These are graphics in the form of line drawings and cartoon-type figures that use solid colors. They are sometimes referred to as *low-memory graphics* because they don't require much file space. A compression technique called Graphic Interchange Format or GIF (officially pronounced as in *jiffy*, but popularly pronounced as in *gift*), is used to save simple graphics in order to make the file sizes smaller and easier to store and transfer.

GIF files contain a maximum of 256 colors, which is not enough to truly represent artwork and photographs that normally contain up to 16.7 million colors.

Most of the newer versions of graphic production software, such as *PowerPoint* and *Corel Draw,* allow graphics to be saved directly in GIF form. Several graphic conversion software packages such as *Graphics Workshop* enable designers to convert figures created in standard graphic forms—like BMP, CGM, PCX, or TIFF—into GIF files.

Artwork and Photographs

The Web can also present graphics in the form of complex artwork and photographs, although not nearly as well as they would appear on paper. The compression technique used for complex graphics on the Web is called JPEG (pronounced *jay-peg*), after the Joint Photographic Expert Group that created the format. Unlike GIF files, which represent graphic information in an 8-bit code, JPEG files can use a 24-bit code that can present the 16.7 million colors necessary to faithfully represent artwork and photographs. However, keep in mind that for users to see all 16.7 million colors, they must have 24-bit display cards and monitors in their systems, otherwise they will be limited to 256 colors. The software used to produce or edit complex graphics usually has the word "photo" in its title and the industry standard is Adobe's *Photoshop.*

Animation

Animations are simple graphics that appear to move: Either a fixed graphic moves from one point to another on the screen, or a graphic gives the impression of motion within its boundaries (for example, an image of a person with legs and arms moving to give the impression of running). There are several methods for producing animations for the Web. The easiest uses *animated* GIFs. This is the equivalent of creating a series of simple graphics on the pages of a pad of paper and then flipping through them quickly to give the impression of motion. The multiple figures can be created on software packages like Macromedia's *Shockwave.* Other software, like *GIF Construction Set Demonstration Page,* produces animated GIFs from a numbered series of individual GIF files.

A second approach to creating animation on the Web is to use a scripting language like JAVA that produces short programs that can be viewed by the most recent generation of browsers. A third approach is to embed a *hyperlink* to a movie file in the Web page. (A hyperlink is a graphic, a "button," or even a piece of text on a Web page that, when "clicked," brings a different part of the page or an entirely different page to the computer screen.) The student clicks on the link and the movie appears on his or her screen. (See *GIF Construction Set Demonstration Page* for sample animations at http://www.mindworkshop.com/alchemy/gcsdemo.html.)

3D Graphics

Both static and dynamic three-dimensional (3D) graphics are now appearing on many Web sites. The static 3D graphics are usually two-dimensional drawings that give the impression of having three dimensions. They are used to give a realistic, full-bodied view of an object, or to provide an impressive logo image for the organizational owner of the Web site. Specialized software like Autodesk 3D *Studio,* Adobe *Photoshop,* and Corel *Draw* is used to create, render, and convert 3D graphics to a Web-based format.

Dynamic 3D graphics are used to support virtual reality worlds on the Web where viewers can choose the perspective from which to view an object, or can move—or even fly through a space—if they wish. A special language called Virtual Reality Modeling Language (VRML) is used to create a Web page with this capability. Of course, the user's browser must be supported by a VRML *plug-in* application in order to view this kind of virtual world. A plug-in (sometimes called a "helper") is a small software program that is run to present specialized kinds of multimedia formats such as sounds and movies.

To construct a virtual world on a Web page (which is not a simple undertaking), one would use a VRML editor such as Caligari's *Fountain,* Silicon Graphic's *WebSpace Author,* or Virtus's 3D *Web Site Builder.* You can see a sample 3D site called *SuperCity 3D Web Pages* at http://vwww.com/hub/3dpage.htm.

Audio and Video

Sounds—including music, narration, and sound effects—and short video clips can also be embedded in a Web site and presented to the viewer. Often, the Web page has a label or graphic indicating that the audio or video clip is available. The label or graphic is a link to a special file on the server, and when the viewer clicks on the link a sound or movie file is downloaded. This can take some time, and the audio or video cannot be heard or viewed until the download is complete. If the viewer's system has the right *player* for the particular type of file (this is often a plug-in helper to the browser), the sound will be heard from the speaker or the video clip will appear in a box on the screen. In the last few years, a process called *streaming* is being used to transport sounds and videos to the client system without the need for downloading. The clip begins immediately and can run for an indefinite time, almost like a radio or television transmission.

The Problem With Multimedia on the Web

Right now, text and graphics are included in all Web-based courses. But what about the other multimedia capabilities such as artwork and photographs, animation, 3D graphics, and audio and video? These multimedia capabilities can provide a perspective existing in certain working conditions—a customer's tone of voice, the speed in which a process is accomplished, the three-dimensional view of a mechanism—that is essential for training mastery or is needed to capture and sustain students' imaginations. These capabilities are now limited because of several major objections to their use:

Limited Display Capabilities of Users

Not all users (that is, potential students in a Web-based course) have computer systems configured to display the more sophisticated multimedia capabilities of the Web. Either their systems do not have the physical attributes such as speed, memory, or resolution or they do not have the appropriate browser or plug-in helper applications necessary to see and hear the display.

Downloading Times

The more extensive multimedia features of the Web often require a long time to be downloaded and displayed on a user's screen. This is especially true when users have slow telecommunications equipment, or there is a great deal of network activity going on at the site of the server or the Internet service provider.

Development Costs

It can require enormous time and effort to acquire or develop the more extensive multimedia techniques and to program them for delivery over the Web. Some people question whether these "bells and whistles" actually add enough value to the learning experience to offset their costs.

Certainly these objections are valid, but a number of counterarguments can be offered in defense of multimedia. Above all, multimedia capabilities should be used judiciously in Web-based instruction. There is a tendency to become dazzled by multimedia's glittering potential, and to incorporate it whether or not it is truly necessary. The designer of a Web-based course must be careful not to fall prey to this, and should take care to limit the application of multimedia to situations in which it will significantly enhance learning.

Practical Tips

When to Use Multimedia

● Does multimedia add real value to the instruction?
● Do students have the appropriate multimedia-ready computer equipment and software?
● Does the speed of the Internet/intranet make multimedia content worth the wait?

Ease of Finding and Installing Helper Applications

Plug-in applications that allow the use of multimedia are readily available on the Web and are often free of charge. Your Web-based instructional materials can provide the students with detailed guidance in locating, downloading, and installing these helper applications. In fact, your materials can provide direct hyperlinks to the Web sites in which the plug-in helper applications are located.

Methods to Speed Up Downloading

Web page designers can do several things to speed up the delivery of multimedia images to students' servers, or to make the wait during downloading more tolerable. They can choose image compression techniques in which the image still looks good, but requires much less memory space and therefore transmits more quickly. They can use formats in which a simple form of the graphic is immediately available on the user's screen and is eventually replaced by the full-bodied image, or in which the image appears right away in a fuzzy form and then slowly emerges to full clarity.

The Web is still in its infancy and its capabilities are rapidly improving. Soon, most of these objections will evaporate. For example, as different types of Web browser software evolve, they include more and more of the common helper applications already built into them. Telecommunication transmission speeds are increasing, streaming technologies are more available, and compression techniques are getting better. Waiting time for downloads is becoming shorter. New software packages are emerging almost every day, which simplify the requirements and reduce the time needed for a novice to produce professional multimedia images.

Web Page Design

Although the content and substance of your distance learning course ought to be the primary consideration, the layout and appearance of your Web pages will have a significant impact on the actions of students. Professionally designed pages help keep students interested. Poorly designed pages interfere with the learning process.

Basic Design Decisions

For the most part, page design is a matter of personal style. There are few absolutes. The Web page is above all a teaching tool, so it should be appealing and easy for students to use. It should not be confusing, overly complex, or so full of gimmicks that it works against your training goals or the efforts of your students.

In fact, there are several controversies raging in the field of page design. With these considerations in mind, here are some of the basic design decisions you will need to make.

Page Length: No Scrolling Versus Scrolling

The argument against scrolling is based on the idea that the material should fit the constraints of the presentation medium. The concept is that amount of information on a page should not go beyond the viewing area of a single computer screen, because if it's not visible on the screen when the page comes up, you can't be sure the student will ever view it. Besides, long pages take longer to download. In this approach, the content should be broken into appropriate-sized chunks, each of which is placed on its own page.

The argument in favor of scrolling says that the length of a page should be determined by the demands of the content. The maximum amount of information on a page should usually exceed the limitations of a computer screen, but should be no longer than two or three screen lengths. The assumption is that because adult learners are used to consuming information in larger than bite-sized chunks, they won't mind scrolling up and down to see all the content. It is also inconvenient for students to print out a whole stack of short, nonscrolling pages.

Frames: Yes or No?

Frames permit the use of two or more Web pages on the same screen, and offer the equivalent of spreading out a number of documents or open folders on your desktop at the same time.

The appeal of frames is that they give the designer wonderful capabilities. One frame can remain relatively fixed, for example, providing the

> **Practical Tips**
>
> # Good Web Page Design
>
> ● Keep it simple—more bells and whistles don't necessarily translate into more effective instruction.
> ● Develop a standard, accessible template.
> ● Limit the need for scrolling; reserve frames for complex navigational requirements.
> ● Consider the browsers of target students—great design is often lost with the use of many types of browsers.

course map, a table of contents, or navigating links, while another provides the content of the course. The designer can also use multiple frames to integrate content from a number of sources, all on the screen at the same time, and all under the control of the student. A sample page making effective use of frames is shown in figure 2.1. The icons in the narrow frame on the left are used for navigation. They always remain in place

Figure 2.1. Page from George Mason University's "Stat Refresher" Web course.

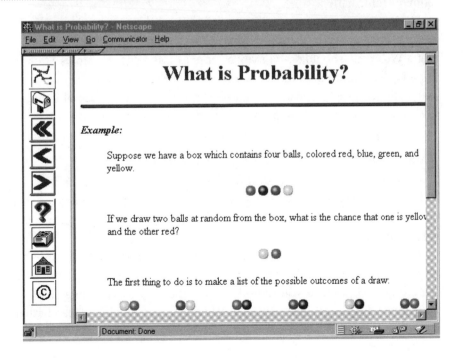

even if the content of the major frame scrolls up or down, left or right, or changes to a different page entirely.

The case against frames is based on the idea that frames look awkward and confuse people. They can break up a screen into such small segments that you have to scroll every which way to see any detail. In addition, not every browser can handle frames, and they can take a very long time to download. Opponents of frames say that almost anything you can do with frames, you can do with other means of Web design, such as *tables.*

For example, the sample page showing the effective use of frames in figure 2.1 could have been produced using a two-column table in which the icons are placed in the narrow column on the left and the remainder of the page in a wide column on the right. The lines forming the table can be made invisible if desired. The only difference between this tables-based page and the previous frame-based page is that the navigational icons would scroll along with the content when using tables.

Special Effects: Use Them Judiciously—or Not at All?

Special effects consist of animation, blinking or scrolling text, sound effects, and other eye-catching and attention-getting features.

The argument for using special effects is that the Web is not just an expedient way to deliver pages of a book to students, but is a vibrant medium of which the designer should take full advantage. Of course you shouldn't overdo it, but special effects can draw attention to critical aspects of the course material, or help to enliven an otherwise dull presentation of information.

Those who advise against using special effects point out that constantly moving images overpower the senses, distract, and annoy. They believe that a Web page should not convey a sense of Las Vegas or Times Square at night, but should give the learner some peace and quiet to read the text and study the graphics. According to this position, creative use of color, layout, typography, and simple graphics is usually sufficient to focus attention on important points while maintaining an air of dignity.

Browser Dependence: Standardize or Customize?

Different types of browsers on students' PCs will react to your page design in different ways. Your pages will look somewhat different for each student depending on the browser they are using and how they have configured it.

As a result, there is one position that says that you should standardize all your Web pages: you've spent a good deal of time and energy to make them look just right, so you should not ruin them by leaving their final appearance to chance. You have several choices if you wish to standardize.

You can prepare your Web pages for the least common denominator. That is, you can determine or prescribe the lowest level of browser capability your students may have (even if it's plain text) and limit the preparation of your Web page to that level.

Another option is that you can require or, if it's practical, equip all students to use the same browser and plug-in helpers, and then design your Web page to be compatible with those applications. A third choice is to convert your Web-based material to a format that is browser independent, such as Portable Document Format (PDF), which is a standardized format for transferring whole pages and documents from one computer to another, and then assure that each student has the appropriate reader available.

You can also customize your Web-based course material, although it will take more time and effort. However, by customizing you can prepare your materials in two ways that will allow it to have a consistent appearance on students' screens. To accomplish this, you merely have to take advantage of the strong points of HTML.

With the first method, your Web page will look virtually the same on each browser. For example, you can define text and the spacing of objects on the screen in such a way that almost all browsers will react to it in the same way and deliver your design or a very close version of it. (In truth, the exact color, font size, and positioning is rarely so terribly important.)

With the second method, students can view the materials in a format that matches the capabilities of their particular browsers. For example, if you know that certain browsers cannot handle frames or certain kinds of graphics, you can prepare the code on your Web page to dictate what students using those browsers will see instead.

It is important for you to think about each of these issues before you begin designing your course materials.

Layout

Good graphic design represents a balance between form (visual sensation) and function (easy access to information). Here are a few layout "absolutes" on which most Web page designers agree.

Use Grids

Provide a basic layout grid or template so that each page has a reasonably predictable look and feel.

Simple Backgrounds

If you don't wish to use the default background, use a background color and pattern that are pale and muted and don't distract the viewer.

Use Headers

Include a header with a prominent title at the top of each page.

Use Appropriate Typography

Be selective in your use of typography—font, type color, size, boldness, underscores, italics, and other attributes.

Use Graphics Carefully

Use only graphics that are critical to the understanding of your content, and try to limit their size, resolution, and number of colors in order to reduce the time for them to appear on the screen.

Use Tables

Use tables to help format your page. They're easy and they're powerful.

● The border lines don't have to be visible.

● You can embed a graphic into a table cell.

● You can change background and border colors.

● Different columns may have a different numbers of rows (and vice-versa).

For example, the sample page in figure 2.2 was created using a table structure with invisible borderlines. The original WordPerfect version showing the actual table structure is in figure 2.3.

Figure 2.2. A table structure with invisible borders.

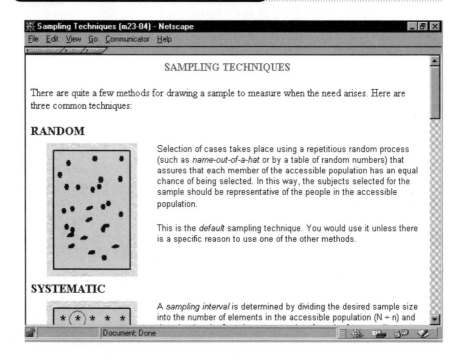

Figure 2.3. Original version of a table structure.

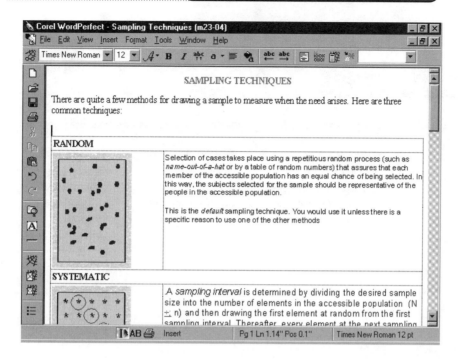

Developing Presentation Materials

Figure 2.4 on page 23 shows a Web page exactly as it is displayed on a student's screen.

Figure 2.5 on page 24 shows the same Web page as it looks in its coded form, defined in HTML coding, with simple graphics represented in a GIF format and artwork and photographs represented in a JPEG format.

How does the designer generate this kind of HTML coding for the Web pages he or she wishes to produce? There are three common approaches.

Direct HTML Coding

Use a simple text writer such as *Notepad* to directly create the HTML coding. Then, save the file with an ".htm" or ".html" extension, depending on the type of Web server being used. (NT type servers use "htm" and UNIX type servers use "html.") Of course, a designer who uses direct HTML coding must know the language inside and out and be confident in the syntax of the language. (See the reference list at the end of this book for the addresses of several free online courses that teach the use of HTML.) If you are not particularly well versed in HTML, the next two methods may be more appropriate for you.

Online Exercise

Connect to the following Web pages and assess the appropriateness of the design decisions and layout of the pages.

Design Characteristics	**Example 1** D-A-D Web Site Services http://www.dipade e.com/Websites/ frames.html	**Example 2** Bicycling Commuting http://www.spies. com/~ceej/Meta/ bike.commuting. html	**Example 3** Glassdog design-o-rama http://www. digiweb.com/ honkzilla/ design-o-rama/
● **Page Length** ○ No scrolling ○ Scrolling			
● **Use of Frames** ○ Yes ○ No			
● **Special Effects** ○ Yes ○ No			
● **Browser Dependence** ○ Yes ○ No			
● **Clear, Clean, Consistent Layout** ○ Yes ○ No			

Figure 2.4. Page from National Defense University's Web course.

Dedicated HTML Editing

There are several products available, including *FrontPage, Hot Dog
Professional,* and *HotMetal Pro,* that are designed to create Web pages
without requiring you to write the HTML tags yourself. Most of them use
menus and drag-and-drop capabilities to construct the necessary coding,
even for frames. They usually include a *WYSIWYG* ("what you see is what
you get") *viewer* so you can see what the page would look like on a
browser. Some allow you to import nontext files such as spreadsheets and
graphics, and automatically convert them to the appropriate Web-based
format. They may have special features, including animation, and techniques for reducing the time necessary to download the page. *FrontPage*
also enables you to transfer the files to your Web server in the appropriate
operating system language. Some knowledge of HTML is useful when you
use a dedicated editor.

Conversion From Word Processors and Authoring Packages

If you have no familiarity with HTML, you may want to use the Web page-
making capabilities in the latest version of the standard word processors,
Word, WordPerfect, and *WordPro.* These have the ability to convert
pages—including both text and graphics—to a Web-based format. You can

Figure 2.5. An example of HTML coding.

Figure 2.5. An example of HTML coding.

```
<HTML>
<HEAD>
  <META HTTP-EQUIV="Content-Type" CONTENT="text/html; charset=iso-8859-1">
  <META NAME="GENERATOR" CONTENT="Mozilla/4.01 [en] (Win95; I) [Netscape]">
  <META NAME="Author" CONTENT="Jay Alden">
  <TITLE>Verifying Expectations {mop32~}</TITLE>
</HEAD>
<BODY TEXT="#000000" BGCOLOR="#C0C0C0" LINK="#0000FF" VLINK="#551A8B"
ALINK="#FF0000">

<CENTER><IMG SRC="mop-banner1.gif" HEIGHT=108 WIDTH=458></CENTER>

<CENTER> </CENTER>

<TABLE BORDER CELLPADDING=5 WIDTH="100%" >
<TR>
<TD VALIGN=TOP WIDTH="50%">
<CENTER><I>Module Three</I> </CENTER>

<CENTER><B>DATA ANALYSIS</B> </CENTER>

<CENTER>Session 2: Verifying Expectations </CENTER>
<IMG SRC="img.gif" HEIGHT=252 WIDTH=285 ALIGN=LEFT></TD>

<TD VALIGN=TOP WIDTH="50%"><A HREF="mop32a.htm"><IMG SRC="img1.gif"
HEIGHT=42 WIDTH=83 ALIGN=BOTTOM></A> 

<P><A HREF="mop32b.htm"><IMG SRC="img2.gif" HEIGHT=42 WIDTH=154 ALIGN=BOT-
TOM></A> 

<P><A HREF="mop32c"><IMG SRC="img3.gif" HEIGHT=42 WIDTH=153 ALIGN=BOT-
TOM></A> 

<P><A HREF="mop32d.htm"><IMG SRC="img4.gif" HEIGHT=42 WIDTH=115 ALIGN=BOT-
TOM></A> 

<P><A HREF="mop32tst.htm"><IMG SRC="img5.gif" HEIGHT=42 WIDTH=175 ALIGN=BOT-
TOM></A> 

<P><A HREF="mop32rf1.htm"><IMG SRC="img6.gif" HEIGHT=42 WIDTH=259 ALIGN=BOT-
TOM></A></TD>
</TR>
</TABLE>
 
</BODY>
</HTML>
```

also use "authoring" packages like *Authorware* and *Director.* With these programs, you first develop a page as you would for printing on paper. Then, instead of printing, you simply select the *"Publish to the Internet"* option (or whatever it is called on that particular software package) and it converts your page into an HTML file. In fact, these software packages have the ability to create the necessary file structure so that the HTML program will know where to find the graphic files. You can also insert hypertext links from any text or graphic on the page to any internal and external locations. At this time, these programs are somewhat slow and most don't handle special capabilities like frames, but you can use them to produce moderately complex Web pages while knowing nothing at all about HTML.

Structure and Navigation

Course Structure

There are many ways in which a Web-based course may be organized. However it is done, it should be systematically structured—and labeled— so that the Web page designer can readily locate individual units, and the students can easily navigate through the materials.

This course has a home page that has hyperlinks to a variety of Web pages containing descriptive materials about the course: Syllabus, Student Evaluation, Course Materials, References and Glossary, and Faculty. The "Course Materials" Web page is a table of contents listing all of the course materials, and each entry in the Contents is a hyperlink to one of the course modules. From this page, the student can link to the first module of any section of the course. (See figure 2.6.)

Each module is composed of one or more pages. Each module may also have links to optional pages containing questions, answers, or further explanations related to the course material.

It is expected that most students will proceed through the course materials (pages, modules, and sections) in numerical order. However, students

Figure 2.6. An example of course organization.

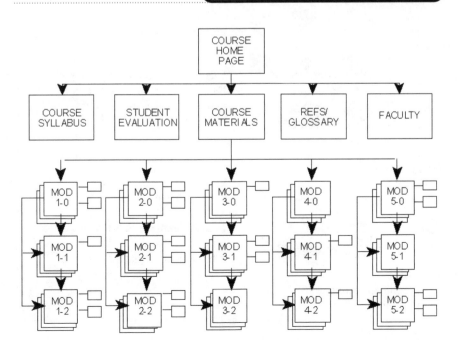

ought to be given the option at any point to go back to any previous point in the course, to skip over a segment they know very well, or to advance to a segment for which they have an immediate need.

Links

With HTML, any word, phrase, graphic, or even part of a graphic may be used as a hyperlink that, when clicked, will send the viewer to another part of the page, another page, or to another Web site. This hyperlinking capability is the very essence of the Web. As noted in the *Web Style Manual*—

> "The ability to mix graphics or motion media with text in HTML is much more limited than in other forms of electronic document

Figure 2.7. Visual elements of a Web page.

Type	Guidelines
Words/Phrases Any word, phrase, or even an entire sentence or paragraph can be made into a link. The textual links appear **highlighted** in some color and possibly underlined (as defined by the viewer's browser).	Keep the number of highlighted words in the link to a minimum, but make them descriptive. Do **not** use the term "Click Here" as the point of the link. Be more descriptive.
Buttons/Graphics Links are often in the form of button boxes… Overview …although any whole graphic can be made into a link…	Reserve *button* links for standardized navigational aids through your material and place them consistently on your page. Use specific titles for text-labels on button links rather than icon-labels and words like "next," which are more ambiguous.
Image Maps Any complex graphic can be made into an image map so that different parts of the graphic are links to different pages or sites.	Clearly delineate the "clickable" regions of an image map. Provide explicit instructions as to what regions should be clicked and what their destinations will be.

authoring, or in paper-based publishing…. However, the ability to embed hypertext links text and graphics that can take full advantage of the Internet offers unprecedented functional power and flexibility in designing interlinked, interactive information systems. Thus page design in HTML should emphasize the power of hypermedia links to take full advantage of this medium." (*Web Style Manual,* Yale Center for Advanced Instructional Media)

There are three visual elements of a Web page that are typically made into active links: words and phrases, buttons and graphics, and image maps. Figure 2.7 explains the basic attributes of each.

For each type of link, the designer should provide sufficient context so the students will know where the link will lead them and why they should go there.

Links can take the students to a wide variety of destinations for any number of instructional purposes. Here are some examples:

Links to another location on the same Web page (Bookmarks)
(See figure 2.8.)

These allow the student to

● advance to the next section of a lesson

● move to a specific segment outlined in a table of contents

● skip over content he or she already knows.

Figure 2.8. A bookmarked link.

Links to another page on the same Web site (See figure 2.9.)

These allow the student to

● do the same things previously listed for *bookmarks*

● transfer to a question, test, or exercise related to the materials just covered

● give the answer or feedback to a question just asked

● switch to a glossary to look up the meaning of a word.

Figure 2.9. Link to a page on the same Web site.

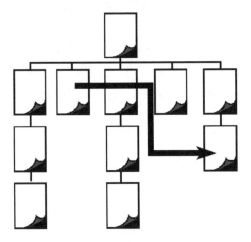

Links to another page on a different Web site (See figure 2.10.)

These enable the student to

● see a demonstration of actual examples of the information just learned

● transfer to referenced sites for further information or specialized training

● go to a search engine to initiate personalized research on the course topic.

Navigation

Navigation is the process of using links to help the students move through the materials that make up a course. Although seemingly straightforward, navigation through a Web-based course is a complex process. Course materials on the Web are usually broken up into hundreds of chunks. A dozen different students may arrive at the same page through a dozen different routes and each might wish to go to a different page when he or she is finished. The

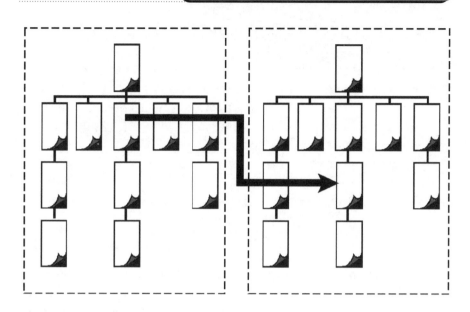

Figure 2.10. Link to a page on a different Web site.

course designer must build in effective navigational support to help each student work his or her own way through the materials. There are four functions used in navigation.

Table of Contents

A Table of Contents (TOC)—with each unit title serving as a link—will enable students to move to any section, module, or even page in the course materials. Sometimes, the TOC includes all the layers of the course structure on a single page, but more often there is a TOC for sections of the course that links to TOCs for modules, and so forth for successively deeper layers of the course.

A single-page TOC can be quite lengthy, but it can be annoying to travel through a structure of multiple-layered TOCs. A few of the more sophisticated distance learning courses produce a TOC in the form of a Course Map (actually an image map). It is recommended that each page in the course include a link back to the TOC. In fact, if the TOC is brief, it could be made part of each page, or placed in a separate frame that is always visible.

Sequence Control

Almost all Web design style guides suggest the use of a standard button bar on each page that allows the students to move to the "Next" page or to return to the "Previous" page in the normal course sequence. (Please note that the "Next" and "Previous" buttons are different from the "Back" and

Practical Tips

Key Factors for Development of Web-Based Instruction

● Work closely with the Webmaster in your organization to identify required formats and appropriate software packages.
● Learn at least the HTML coding basics so you can override errors of Web page editors.
● Use image maps sparingly.
● Make sure students can easily navigate through the course and can always return to a table of contents.
● Test your Web-based instruction on your students' browsers so at least 90 percent will have a problem-free experience.

"Forward" buttons on the browser that move you back and forth along the path—which is different from the typical course sequence—that you took to get to the current page. (See the following section on Retracing Steps.) The style guides differ about where to place the "Next" and "Previous" buttons on the page, and how to label them. Some say to put them on top, others on the bottom, others on the top *and* bottom if the page is long. You can even put them in a frame on the side. It really doesn't matter where you put them, as long as the placement is consistent.

Some style guides recommend using the words "Next" and "Previous" on the buttons, or using symbolic icons—such as a turning page—to represent direction. Others, however, say this can be ambiguous and that the links should be supported with specific references, for example, "To Module 3-2." Another suggestion is that long pages should include a link back to the top of the page.

Side Trips

Both the beauty and woe of Web-based courses is that the students can take excursions into hyperspace. Besides referring students to internal resources—reviews of information previously covered, enrichment information in a kind of appendix, a glossary of terms, an elaborate graphic— course material can refer them to a whole external world out on the Web, full of additional information related to the course. If you provide a link to those sources, some students will take the trip. The question is, will they be able to get back? (See figure 2.11.)

Figure 2.11. HTML code preparation.

Retracing Steps

Table of Contents

Sequence Control

Side Trips

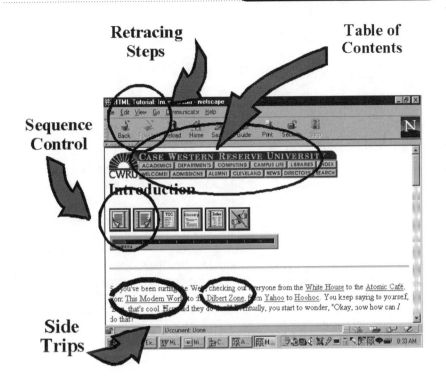

To help them decide whether or not to take the trip, you should supplement the link with explicit information about where they will be going and what they will see when they get there. Some designers also provide information on the relative size of the referenced page so they will know how much time the trip will take. It is also recommended that your design allow students to be able to distinguish between references to internal and external pages.

Retracing Steps

All browsers provide "Back" and "Forward" buttons that allow students to move backward and forward along the path through pages they have already taken. For example, if they took a side trip to an external reference you provided, they can get back to your page using the "Back" button. As a course designer, there is nothing you can do to change the operation of these buttons, but you can make sure that your students can distinguish their function from any "Next" and "Previous" buttons you might provide.

Online Exercise

Connect to the following Web pages and assess the appropriateness of the form of the links and their destinations, and the quality of the navigational aids:

	Example 1 Maricopa Center for Learning and Instruction, Writing HTML: A tutorial for creating WWW pages http://www.mcli. dist.maricopa.edu/ tut/lessons.html	**Example 2** Defense Acquisition University Stat Refresher http://www2-cne.gmu.edu/ modules/dau/stat/ dau2_frm.html	**Example 3** Pennsylvania State University Case Studies in Turf Management http://www.cas. psu.edu/docs/ casdept/turf/turf 436/turf436.html
• **Use of Links**			
• **Form of Links**			
• **Link Destinations**			
• **Navigational Support**			

Chapter 3. Student Interaction

Interaction is as crucial for online instruction as it is for any other kind of teaching, perhaps more so. In fact, online instruction may offer richer opportunities and make stronger demands for student interaction than other types of instruction.

Types of Interactions

Students in online courses can interact in four ways: with materials, with the instructor, with other students, and with subject matter experts. Not every Web-based course will offer all four types of interaction, but the more types that are used, the more effective the course will be.

Students Interacting With Materials

In online courses, students interact with instructional materials the same way they would with computer-based instruction. They can be asked multiple-choice questions and be given personalized feedback based on their answers. They can be asked to identify a specific part of a graphic image, and be told immediately whether or not they chose correctly. They can be asked to fill in a form, participate in a simulation, fly a spaceship—all without any need for the intervention of a live instructor.

Students Interacting With the Instructor

Online students can interact individually with their instructor in the same way they would in a classroom. The instructor can ask a question of the entire group of students and wait for someone to answer. The instructor can direct a question to a particular student—in public or in private—and obtain an immediate top-of-the-head response or a longer, more considered response. Students have the same ability to ask questions of the instructor and receive an individual response. Students can submit lengthy papers or projects for review or grading, and then receive individual feedback. They can also be counseled by the instructor in private.

Students Interacting With Other Students

Online students can work together on projects or in small group exercises, either under the watchful eye of the instructor or on their own, in private.

A pair of students or a larger group can engage in a bull session about the course content. The instructor can facilitate discussions by the full class or among special interest groups—asking probing questions, clarifying and summarizing, and keeping the focus on the discussion topic.

Students Interacting With Subject Matter Experts

Online students have the unique capability to query outside experts to answer questions or to gain a different perspective based on the expert's special experience. In a way, this is equivalent to having a guest speaker in the classroom, but the question-and-answer session is much more personal. Although it is possible for students to ask questions of any expert whose e-mail address they know, this type of interaction works best when the instructor gains the advance commitment of experts who agree to answer student questions.

Interacting Without Computers

Each of the four types of interactions can also take place without the use of computers. Standard mail and telephone services will probably continue to be used in the foreseeable future to support distance learning.

Standard Mail

Often, it is much faster and cheaper to prepare noninteractive reference materials or large, complex graphics in book form and ship them to the students before a course begins. Sometimes it is easier on the students if the courseware is placed on a CD-ROM and mailed to them instead of asking them to download the materials from the Web. If student project papers can be submitted by mail rather than by telecommunications, network and system requirements can be reduced.

Telephone

If an instructor and a student need to talk about a complex concept, it is often much easier to pick up the telephone. A group discussion can work perfectly well with a conference call instead of an online session, and students who have limited e-mail systems can fax project papers to the instructor.

Interactive Computer Technologies

In online courses, interaction primarily makes use of quicker and often less expensive computer technologies including programmed software, e-mail, mailing lists, asynchronous computer conferencing, and synchronous chat. This section will concentrate on the more common computer technologies, which are most often applied with the text and simple

graphics used to provide interactions in relatively low-budget online courses. The more expensive and vibrant multimedia interactive technologies
may also be mentioned as a possible instructional enrichment.

Programmed Software

For part or even all of a Web-based course, students might interact with
the course materials without the intervention of an instructor, or discussion
with other students. Because the student basically works alone, this type
of online coursework operates similarly to stand-alone computer-based
instruction courses that are distributed over the Web. There are currently
two common techniques for building programmed interactions into online
courses: hyperlinking and *interactive forms*.

Hyperlinking

The course designer uses the hyperlinking referencing technique in
HTML, as described in chapter two. A question is presented, for which
each possible answer is linked to a page with specific feedback for that
particular answer.

On the feedback page, the course designer might provide feedback and
an explanation, or as in figure 3.1, give the student more choices and link
each selection to an appropriate page.

Figure 3.1. Hyperlinking.

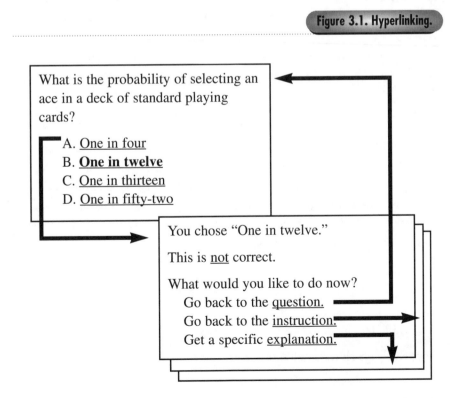

Figure 3.2. An image map.

Click on the state of Arkansas?

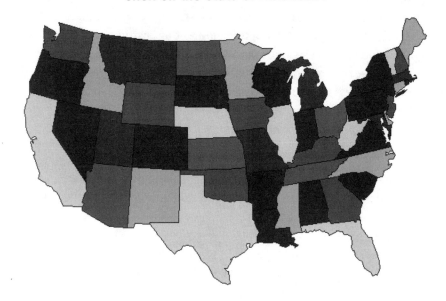

Image Maps

Image maps can also be used in hyperlinking interactions. Remember, a designer can graphically segment any portion of a figure and then have each section link to a different Web page. Of course, an image map does not have to be a representation of an actual map, as in figure 3.2. For example, it might be a graphic or photograph of a machine, which would display more detailed information like specifications or an exploded view when the student clicks a particular part of the machine.

One cautionary note: since each information page, question page, and feedback page is usually retained in a separate file, the challenge to the developer of the Web-based materials in this approach is keeping track of all the possible paths through the files. Usually, a good numerical-based organizing scheme or a graphical course map similar to that used in computer-based instruction will work.

Interactive Forms

Using HTML, the course designer can develop a form that the student must complete. The form can serve as a quiz or exam, or as a study and review aid. The form can use many types of features such as

- boxes in which the student can type a response

- boxes with a pull-down menu of options the student can select

- radio-style buttons next to options that the student can select.

When the student completes the form, he or she clicks a button that says "submit form," and the answers are processed. This happens most commonly in an interaction between the student's browser and the Web server: Clicking the "submit" button sends the entries on the form from the browser on the student's client system to the Web server. (See figure 3.3.)

The server software typically includes a Common Gateway Interface (CGI) script that processes the entries. (The CGI script is written in a Unix-based programming language called Perl.) For example, the script might compare the student's answers against the correct answers, derive a numerical score, and create an appropriate feedback message for the student. The score can be sent to a record-keeping application and the feedback message sent back to the student's browser as in figure 3.4.

Currently, the JAVA language (which, like HTML, works the same way on any kind of computer system) is being used more and more to process

Figure 3.3. An interactive form.

Self-Test

Name: [   ]   **Class:** [   ]

Please select the appropriate answer for all questions and then click the *submit exam for grading* button.

1. If a fair die is rolled, what is the probability of five turning up?	**2.** What is the probability that two tails come up if two fair coins are tossed?	**3.** What is the probability of one showing up at least once in two tosses of a fair die?
○ A. 0 ○ B. 1 ○ C. 1/6 ○ D. 2/6	○ A. 1/2 ○ B. 1/4 ○ C. 3/4 ○ D. 3/2	○ A. 1 ○ B. 1/36 ○ C. 11 ○ D. 11/36

Submit exam for grading	**Reset answers**

Figure 3.4. A Common Gateway Interface (CGI).

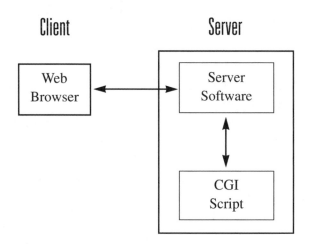

interactive forms. A small computer program called an "applet" that processes the information on the form is written using JAVA by someone knowledgeable in that language. The processing program is downloaded to the browser at the same time as the form, so the processing takes place right away at the student's computer without involving the server. This results in faster and slicker feedback, which can include animation and other effects as well as text.

A Web-based instruction course that relies almost solely on programmed software is really a computer-based training (CBT) course delivered over the Web. Use this approach when the training content involves very prescriptive step-by-step kinds of tasks where there are single right answers to questions. If you can restrict interaction just to programmed software, you can significantly cut costs and time for delivering the instruction. Student-to-instructor ratios of a few hundred-to-one are not unusual with Web-based CBT. Of course, you would also increase the development costs since, to keep the students interested, you must make the programmed interactions graphical, colorful, and creative—even gamelike—if at all possible.

Programmed software is less useful when the training content involves soft skills, tasks that require a great deal of interpretation and judgment, and for which there are many "right" answers. In these cases, direct instructor involvement is often required to interpret student responses. One expedient technique to hold down instructor activity in Web-based soft skills training is to provide a link from an open-ended question or student exercise in the course materials to a so-called "school answer"—a complex response that provides a sample good answer with enough explanation for the students to judge their own responses. Suggest that the students then check the "school answer" after they have constructed a response to the question.

E-mail

E-mail is probably the most universally available form of one-on-one electronic communications for students. A student or instructor creates and sends a message individually to another student or instructor who can send a reply in turn. It's relatively quick and personal and is the equivalent of having a private conversation. E-mail is also an example of a push strategy, because the person receiving the message doesn't have to do much to get it: the message is *pushed* his or her way and shows up at his or her doorstep. Most e-mail systems useful for distance learning have several capabilities:

● They provide a reply mechanism to allow the respondent easily to send a message back to the sender.

● They encode and decode attachments to the message so that materials developed with other software applications (word processing, graphics, spreadsheets) can be sent and viewed by the receiver, if they have the same software application.

● They allow the receiver easily to set up an archive of designated files in order to save messages according to their topical category.

In Web-based courses that are severely constrained by technology or budget, e-mail is the primary means of course instruction. The instructor sends information and questions to individual students, and the students respond. Students also converse one-on-one with each other the same way.

However, in most Web-based courses, e-mail is typically an adjunct to other means of instruction. It is usually reserved for private conversations between individual students and with the instructor or guest experts.

Mailing Lists

A mailing list is an extension of the e-mail capability. It allows an individual to simultaneously send the same message to a large number of people, all of whom are on the mailing list. In this way, it is a convenience that saves the sender from having to enter a large number of addresses in the "TO:" box of the e-mail system.

Brute Force

The brute force method for setting up a mailing list is to have every student and faculty member create and save a list, on his or her own system, with the name and e-mail address of every person associated with the distance learning course. (This assumes everyone's e-mail system has

this capability.) They must do this only one time, and they then assign this list a group name. From then on, when they post a message using the group name of that list of addresses, everyone on the list will get a copy of the message. A problem with this approach is that if the list has to change for any reason (if, for example, someone is dropped from or added to the course roster), everyone on the list has to revise his or her own mailing list.

Mailing List Packages

A more common approach is to place on a server a specialized piece of mailing list administration software, often called a *listserv,* which can automatically create and maintain the list of addresses. Some of the more common listserv packages are *Mailserv, ListProc,* and *Majordomo.* These mailing list packages can provide a number of features.

One feature is moderation: a mailing list may be *moderated or unmoderated.* With a moderated list, a designated person first screens all messages sent to the list. The moderator must approve a message before it is actually posted to the list, and can screen out duplications and inappropriate or offensive messages. The moderator can also edit and add comments to messages. In unmoderated lists, messages sent by list members are automatically posted to the list.

Archives are another feature. The messages sent to a list may be stored in an archive. This way, list members will be able to review messages they have previously deleted, and can gain access to the past history of all messages sent to the mailing list. The archive may be organized in any number of ways and may have a search feature to help members locate particular messages.

Mailing lists can also be automated—set up so that members can automatically be subscribed or unsubscribed, post messages, temporarily stop and resume getting messages, and access the archives—all without the list administrator's involvement. The only requirement is that members know the commands they need to use for the various list functions. For example, some mailing lists provide the option of a *digest,* which allows members to get, in a single e-mail transmission, all messages posted to the list in a given day. They can send the list a particular command to begin or stop using that form of message transmission.

Web Conferencing

Web conferencing is a common way to interact in distance learning courses. This approach is similar to mailing lists because messages from students or faculty can be viewed by everyone in the group. Web conferencing differs from mailing lists in that the messages are not transmitted to the viewer's e-mail system. Rather, they are posted and viewed on a Web page that can be accessed by all members of the group. In other words, Web conferencing uses a *pull strategy*—the viewer must take action and go to the Web page to get the information. This is the opposite of the push strategy of a mailing list, on which the messages are delivered to the viewers whether they want them or not. Web conferencing is similar to electronic bulletin boards and news groups that are used for asynchronous computer communication.

Web Conferencing Software Capabilities

Using special Web conferencing software packages on servers, the course designer organizes a hierarchical structure where messages can be posted. The highest level is a *conference group,* which might encompass a particular course or a class within that course. Under this group, the course designer may set up a number of *topical areas* (different course modules, issues, or administrative functions), to which instructors or students may post messages. In fact, once messages are posted other people can respond directly to them and several members can conduct a conversation.

Figure 3.5 shows a table of contents of conversations in the topical area devoted to questions and answers about JAVA language from a course called "WWW Programming" at the University of North Carolina. A member of the class can view any message in the table of contents by clicking on its title. If the viewer would like to respond to one of these messages, he or she would click on "Post Message" among the options running across the screen above the table of contents, and a message form would appear on the screen. The viewer could complete the form and click on a "submit" button within the form: the message would then be posted to this site for all to view, and its title would show up in the table of contents.

Most Web conferencing software packages give any member of the conference the ability to start his or her own thread of conversation under any topical area. However, the conference administrator usually has the ability to control the level at which users may begin threads. In most online courses, Web conferencing is used for structured discussions set up by the instructor to supplement the course instruction. For example, an instructor may set up one topic for each of 10 modules. A student is prevented from starting an eleventh discussion topic at the same level of the 10 modules. The topics are set up for particular course modules, projects, or probing questions. There are often other noninstructional topics set aside for administrative issues, special interest areas, or informal coffee-break discussions. Groups of students may also use their own Web conference to discuss team projects. This could be set up independently by the students or by the instructor, depending on the capabilities of the conferencing package and the instructor's preference.

Figure 3.5. A Web conference topical site on JAVA.

Comp 190—Section 025—Spring 1997

Java Q&A

....

[Post Message] [Archive] [Back to Forums for this Course] [Return to Course Homepage]

● Java evaluation of boolean expressions—**Dug** 00:53:13 04/09/97 (0)
● Java is frustrating!!!!!!!!!!!—**Noel** 10:37:19 04/07/97 (0)
● Interfacing between classes—**Dug** 00:12:18 03/09/97 (0)
● Creating a string to a float?—**Chris** 00:59:43 03/01/97 (1)
  ○ Re: Casting a string to a float?—**Gary** 11:47:15 03/02/97 (0)
● Server port reservation on capefear—**Noel** 20:13:42 02/27/97 (2)
  ○ Re: Server port reservation on capefear—**jbs** 09:18:13 03/01/97 (1)
    ■ Re: Re: Server port reservation on capefear—**Noel** 10:44:55 03/03/97 (0)
● Defining more than one class in a file—**Jeff** 20:47:26 02/26/97 (1)
  ○ Re: Defining more than one class in a file—**Noel** 20:09:26 02/27/97 (0)
● Passing parameters to an Applet—**Mark** 10:15:35 02/22/97 (2)
  ○ Re: Passing parameters to an Applet—**Sam** 01:41:50 02/24/97 (1)

Software Types

There is an enormous choice of Web conferencing software. Some common packages are called *Caucus, Forum, HyperNews, Lotus Domino, Podium,* and *Web Crossing.* Some programs will run only on servers that operate with UNIX, others only on servers with Windows NT/95, and a few will run on both. They vary in price from free shareware to proprietary packages costing several thousand dollars. All of them handle text messages, but a few of the more expensive software packages will have the capability for *attachment handling,* which means that they will accommodate postings that include graphics and attachments produced under other software applications. Some packages will also permit *collaborative groupwork,* which enables all the members of a team to add to or edit the same posted document or attachment.

Synchronous Chat

Web conferencing has many benefits, but its downside is that the communications often lack a feeling of spontaneity and energy. However, there is an option called *synchronous chat* that can capture the benefits of the best of lively class discussions in an online environment, and that offers interactions that are stimulating, synergistic, insightful, and fun. Synchronous chat works a little like Web conferencing, except that the group logs on at the same time—just as the students in a live class all sit together with the instructor—and the postings are made about just one conference topic.

In text-based chat systems, messages from the participants appear on the screen in real time soon after they are submitted in the order in which they are received by the server. Typically, the name or ID of the person submitting the message is listed alongside his or her submission. In heated discussions, the entries come in one right after the other at a frenzied pace, causing the screen to continuously scroll upward. (See figure 3.6.)

There are thousands of synchronous chat servers available through the Web that will allow you to engage in discussion on any topic. When a training or educational institution uses synchronous chat to support distance learning, it either has its own chat server software or it uses the chat server capabilities of a vendor. Synchronous chats are used in Web-based instruction in the same way that Web conferencing is used. The instructor leads

Figure 3.6. A synchronous chat screen.

Instructor:	Why would an organization OBJECT to measuring the "impact" of its own performance?
Student 07:	It may not be in its political interests.
Student 13:	The organization might have little control over how its customers use its products and services and doesn't want to be held responsible for something it can't control.
Student 05:	What do you mean—political interests?
Student 14:	They could get beaten up if the impact isn't positive. If the results are too good, management may think they're over-resourced and cut their budget.
Student 07:	By political interests, I mean their ability to retain their resources and to control their own destiny.

discussions on course topics, and the students participate. Students can also use the synchronous chat for team projects or informal discussions on any topic they choose.

Software for Synchronous Chat

Client software for synchronous chat is often free, but server software, which is rich in special features, can be expensive, costing $10,000 or more. Almost all this software is compatible with the Internet Relay Chat (IRC) standard. Many of these software programs will work with standard browsers, but some require that the user have special software or browser plug-ins. The special software often provides additional discussion capabilities including file transfers, hyperlinks, voice, encryption, whiteboards, and 3D graphics. Two examples of sophisticated Web software are Quarterdeck's *Global Chat* (www.globalchat.com) and *Ichat's Rooms* (www.ichat.com). With *Global Chat,* group membership can be restricted to particular people, users can create their own groups, and transcripts of meetings can be recorded. With *Rooms,* any visitor to a Web page can communicate in real time with any other site visitor. *Rooms* also supports banners, ticker-tape marquees, and even virtual reality-based spaces and customizable *avatars* (graphic figures representing the users). Both packages allow the instructor to moderate.

Virtual Office Hours

Some instructors have used synchronous chat to hold "virtual office hours." For one or two hours a week, the instructor logs into the chat room and is available to field questions from any student on any topic. Some instructors also use the chats to conduct review sessions of course modules. In some courses in which team projects are a major requirement, a chat room is set up and scheduled for particular groups of students to work out the details without moderation by the instructor.

Downsides of Synchronous Chat

There are some downsides to synchronous chat. As in live classroom discourses, the discussion can be dominated by those who think fast. Unlike classroom discussions, chat also favors those who type quickly. There is a belief that people who are quiet in face-to-face discussions will "speak up" more readily in a text-based chat session, but there is little evidence to support this. And, as with all types of electronic communication, users may need extensive training before the systems become second nature and easy to use.

Practical Tips

How to Minimize Problems With Student Interaction on the Web

● E-mail is by far the most risk-free means of communication—almost everyone can use it.
● Most servers provide a built-in conferencing capability using "news-groups," but students have to be instructed in the procedure to subscribe to your news group and many organizations' firewalls often restrict access to newsgroups over the Internet. (They work fine over an intranet.)
● Don't use both a mailing list and Web conferencing. They serve a similar purpose and the fewer new software packages students have to learn, the better.
● Chat sessions have to be scheduled—they almost never spring up spontaneously.
● Keep the time zones of the various students in mind when scheduling a chat session.

Collaboration

Training classes for higher-level employees such as managers and senior-level professionals often require small-group exercises in which the students collaborate on team projects, reflecting their work in meetings and on special project teams or task forces. In classroom courses, these exercises usually involve the use of breakout rooms or after-hours assignments.

Web-based instructional courses may also require students to work together in small groups, either synchronously or asynchronously, on joint projects. To do this effectively, the software should enable student teams to participate in the kinds of activities that frequently occur during meetings. Ideally, the software should enable students to

● share a common working space called a virtual whiteboard, which might contain a project such as a spreadsheet, graphic, document, or virtually any kind of software application for which each student in the common working space may contribute

● communicate with each other to suggest ideas, pose questions or answers, provide clarification, indicate agreement or disagreement, or vote on an issue

• during the meeting, manage, share (through file transfer), archive, search, and navigate through information resources such as technical references, policy documents, and minutes of previous meetings.

Some of the more advanced Web conferencing and synchronous chat software discussed earlier can deliver many of these functions. There are also specialized software packages designed especially to support group collaboration. WebBoard from O'Reilly & Associates (www.ora.com), *NetMeeting* from Microsoft (www.microsoft.com/), and *Domino* (www.lotus.com/) are three highly rated packages. At the very least, the collaboration software should enable the instructor to set up work spaces where groups of students can work together on projects and team members can see the project being worked on. In some packages, every team member can make changes to the product; in others, changes must be sent to the one team member who controls the product. The better systems allow all team members to view specialized computer applications (for example, a particular kind of spreadsheet), even if that software is not resident on their PCs. A number of collaboration software packages include audioconferencing or even desktop videoconferencing capabilities, so that the team members can actually hear and see each other as they work.

Simulations

Perhaps the most complex of all instructional interactions involves simulations. In classroom simulations, students are artificially placed in difficult circumstances that look and feel very realistic. These situations change in accordance with evolving events, only some of which the students control. The simulation typically continues until the student obtains a correct solution, fails, or time runs out. Online simulations are expensive to develop, but two broad types have been used with online courses.

Model-Based Simulations

Think of the computer game *Flight Simulator.* A designer develops a dynamic model as in figure 3.7 (complete with inputs, processes, and outputs), of some apparatus or operation. The model is created with the help of a software application like *Toolbook II* that can represent the model's outward appearance and internal functioning. The software package can also transform the model into formats that are compatible with the Web, such as HTML, VRML, GIF, JPEG, and JAVA.

Typically, the complete model resides on the server, and parts are downloaded to the student's client system to make the model's attributes visible, often using animation, 3D graphics, and even virtual reality (VR). As the student interacts with the model by clicking on objects, clicking and dragging, or entering data in the right places, his or her inputs are processed

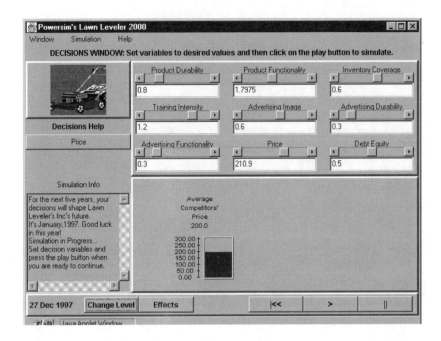

and transformed into physical changes on the screen. (See figure 3.8.) The student's actions and the simulation's reactions continue until the simulation is finished—when time runs out or the results are achieved.

Group-Based Simulations

This is a form of *role playing,* conducted online. The designer develops a scenario describing a difficult situation that one or more people might face. The designer also establishes and assigns roles that different students assume in dealing with this situation. Instructions for playing the roles can be sent to the individual students confidentially, by e-mail. The simulation can begin with a signal from the instructor, who will continually monitor the action. In its simplest form, the simulation is conducted using a synchronous chat or, less often, by Web conferencing. This type of simulation is dynamic, and the role players interact verbally with each other. The intensity of the interaction can be heightened by using collaborative groupware, like a whiteboard, or even a shared simulated space in which each player is represented by an avatar. It is even possible to use actual voices. The simulation continues until the players reach an agreement, the instructor intervenes, or time runs out.

Figure 3.8. An effects screen from a model-based simulation.

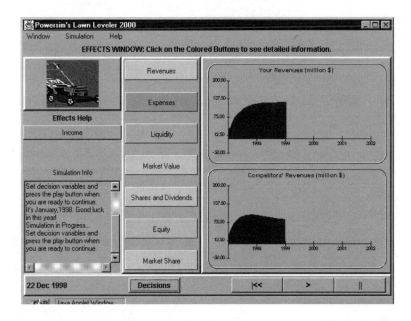

Combined Simulations (MUDs and MOOs)

The combination of these two types of simulations (groups of people interacting with each other and a model) is often referred to as a MUD (Multi-User Domain/Dimension/ Dungeon) or MOO (MUD Object Oriented). Right now, most MOOs and MUDs are primarily text-based systems used for social interactions and games. But more of them are being introduced into 3D virtual worlds where users can construct additions according to designated rules (see www.thepalace.com and www.superscape.com). Sometime soon, they should evolve into highly sophisticated models that can be used for simulations in Web-based instruction.

Online Exercise

Use these online programs to gain some hands-on practice with some of the interactive techniques described in this chapter.

- **Programmed Software**

  Connect to the *virtualvegas* home page (www.virtualvegas.com). Choose "Casino Games" and take advantage of the free registration. Play both the JAVA-based blackjack game (that downloads a JAVA applet one time to your computer before the series of games are played), and the classic blackjack game (that uses CGI scripting at the server location and requires communication between your computer and the server during each play of each game). Note the professionalism of the graphics as well as the relative speed and smoothness in the way your selections are processed in each game.

- **Web Conferencing**

  Connect to the home page of *The Center@Hamline* (http://center.hamline.edu). Hamline University in St. Paul, Minnesota, runs a public Web conference (using the Caucus software package) that covers distance learning and other topics. Register as a user (it's free) and join in one of the available discussions that interests you. You can even set up your own discussion thread if you wish.

- **Synchronous Chat**

  Connect to the *Human Services Chat Net* (www.naswnm.org/chat/index.html). The site uses a software product called *Chat Touring* that makes use of JAVA applets. This particular product also lets users share documents while they are chatting. Enter either the *Conference Room* or the *CyberCafe* to experience text-based chats.

- **Simulation**

  Connect to Powersim Corporation's site to run a simulation of "flying" a hot air balloon (http://www.powersim.no/WebSims/HotAir/). This is what Powersim calls a "WebSim"—where you control the burning device of a hot air balloon. Your mission is to make the balloon airborne and land it neatly near or on the target on the ground. A JAVA applet first downloads the graphics and processing scripts that react to the user's operational decisions—how long to burn, how much gas to release, and how much weight to drop. When you start the simulation, you see a host of readings such as vertical speed and altitude of the hot air balloon, and a view of the balloon against a choice of backgrounds. The simulation plays out until you land the balloon with a soft landing and using the least amount of gas. Your final score is then compared with other flyers' results.

Chapter 4. Course Management

Management Activities

Although the management of Web-based courses is similar in many ways to the management of classroom courses, it differs significantly in several areas.

Scheduling the Course

Classroom instruction tends to be scheduled in a "batch" mode. That is, a group of students starts the course at the same time and progresses through it in a lockstep fashion. Most Web-based courses are currently scheduled in the same way. Although the pacing and perhaps the sequencing are more individualized, all the online students in a given course tend to begin and move through the course on roughly the same schedule. As a result, online instructors can regularly send out introductory messages or minilectures as each module is reached, and chat sessions on particular topics can be scheduled when the student groups are ready for them.

As explained in chapter 1, one major difference between online and classroom courses is that Web-based asynchronous courses typically require up to 30 times as much time as classroom courses. That is, a training course that requires three consecutive days in a classroom setting may require up to three months to complete when students can log in at any time from any place. The online students and instructors put in about the same amount of time on the coursework as a classroom course (perhaps a bit more because of all the opportunities for interaction described in the previous chapter); it is just spread out over a longer period.

Some experienced Web-based instructors ask, "Why not take full advantage of the medium and arrange the course for *just-in-time learning?* They suggest that students be permitted to start the courses whenever they want—three one day, one a few days later, two a week after that, and so on. The instructor's introductory messages for each module can be available on a Web conference whenever the student is ready for them. Chats on particular topics can be scheduled periodically and those students who are interested can participate. This way, students can begin the training just when they need it and when it is convenient. Of course, instructors in such scheduling scenarios have to be adept at moving through the course content, stopping and reversing, or changing direction on a dime. The just-in-time approach works particularly well when most of the interaction is programmed, or when the instructor has built up a library of canned responses to typical student questions (perhaps publishing them online in a set of *frequently asked questions* or *FAQs.*)

Selecting and Developing Faculty

Most institutions that introduce distance learning plan to use their current classroom faculty as the online instructors. At first glance, this seems to make sense: take experienced, effective classroom instructors, equip them with the skills to use the software, and presto!, you have qualified online instructors, ready for action.

Well, some authorities on distance learning don't think so. They believe that the teaching skills required for classroom instruction do not directly transfer to online instruction. They question whether the personality and motivation of the outstanding classroom teacher are the same as those that make an excellent online instructor. These are legitimate concerns because there are some significant differences between the two types of teaching.

Qualities Required of Online Instructors

Successful online instructors need four critical talents and skills, which differ from those that make a successful classroom instructor.

● **Technology Competence.** An online instructor must be capable and comfortable using computer hardware and software. Although computer technology is becoming easier to use, conducting—and especially developing—Web-based courses requires an instructor who enjoys learning about and using advanced technology. The Web is no place for a technophobic instructor who cringes at the sight of a keyboard.

Practical Tips

Choosing Online Instructors—Top Four Criteria

- genuine interest and competence in technology
- ability to converse using a keyboard
- enjoyment from coaching students more than performing for them
- does not teach using only a step-by-step linear fashion.

- **Facility With Written Language.** Most online communication is through written words and graphics. In contrast, a classroom environment allows an instructor to take advantage of his or her skill in the art of speech. Most of us know people who excel in one of these types of verbal communication, but not in the other. Web-based instructors must be able to express themselves effectively (and quickly) through written language.

- **Teaching Style.** As we saw in chapter 3, interaction is the essence of Web-based instruction. The online instructor is primarily a facilitator who helps students progress through the course by steering, advising, questioning, and giving feedback. The same strategy is effective in the classroom. However, some classroom instructors enjoy the performance aspect of teaching as much as the instruction. They see themselves as the center of attraction, the fountain of information who enlightens the students. A few charismatic people do seem to have the extraordinary ability to teach by lecturing, but most don't. The "sage on the stage" mentality doesn't easily make the transition to Web-based instruction. A more appropriate model is the "coach on the sidelines."

- **Adaptability.** It is said that with asynchronous Web-based instruction, a faculty member does not conduct one class of 20 students; rather, he or she has 20 classes of one student each, all going at the same time. Online instructors spend a great deal of time working with and responding to individual students or teams of students. Unlike classroom teaching, Web-based instruction tends to be nonlinear from the teacher's perspective. Within a short time period, the online instructor might advise one student on an appropriate project for Module 7, then switch to providing feedback on another student's paper from Module 4, and then offer suggestions to yet another student about useful references for an exercise from Module 8. An online instructor must be able to shift gears quickly and easily.

Capabilities Required of Online Faculty

If, as is often the case, online faculty members are chosen based not on personality and style, but primarily on expertise in the subject matter of the course, then faculty development becomes essential. Candidates for online faculty should be carefully selected and well trained and should already have several basic skills and abilities such as the following:

- proficiency in Web-based software applications used in the course

- ability to present information in a way that promotes interactions with and among students

- ability to manage the course according to the dictates of the software

• fluency in the strategies of Web-based instruction, so they will be at ease navigating through multiple online learning resources, which is an extremely important asset

• facility for encouraging extensive interaction between students and the materials, the instructor, the other students, and subject matter experts

• ability to create opportunities for collaborative learning and work among teams of students

• capacity to serve more as a facilitator than as a single source of knowledge

• a strong belief in the efficacy of Web-based instruction. A candidate for the online faculty should not consider Web-based instruction merely as a backup for classroom teaching when it is inconvenient or impractical to bring students together at the same time and place. Instructors should be convinced that Web-based instruction offers valuable capabilities beyond the constraints of an ordinary classroom.

How can you develop such an enthusiastic Web-based instructor? Certainly, if the training institution is large enough, it should consider creating its own faculty development course on Web-based instruction, customized to its own approach. If the institution cannot embark on such an ambitious undertaking, there are a number of vendors who conduct conferences and workshops on the topic. If you belong to a professional association like the American Society for Training & Development, you probably receive fliers and brochures advertising such conferences.

Of course, it will be even more effective if that course on Web-based instruction is conducted completely or partially online. What better way to learn about Web-based instruction than to experience it firsthand? In fact, whether or not instructors attend a workshop specifically about Web-based instruction, they should try to take as many online courses on as many topics as they can. There are hundreds of online courses available on the Web, many of them free of charge. A few courses related to developing Web-based instruction are listed in the reference section at the end of this book, but you can conduct a search of the Web yourself by including the name of a topic of interest and the key words "online" and "training" in your search. (A typical search might look like this: business writing + online + training.)

Developing online instructors need to experience as many varieties of Web-based instruction as possible to see what works well and what doesn't. It also pays to experiment by first developing a few lessons on any topic and conducting them online with friends and colleagues who will provide candid feedback. Joining listservs related to distance learning and actively participating in discussions about the strategies, benefits, and risks of Web-based instruction will also help you to develop a deep understanding of the process. Two particularly useful listservs are the DEOS-L listserv managed by Pennsylvania State University (deos-l@lists.psu.edu), which has a primarily scholarly orientation and the WWWDEV listserv run by the University of New Brunswick (wwwdev@listserv.unb.ca), which has a primarily "nuts and bolts" technical orientation.

Gaining Student Participation

There are always some students in classroom courses who rarely participate. They do the required exercises, but they never ask or voluntarily answer the instructor's questions. At least instructors can see them and read their facial expressions and body language, so they can tell if these students are paying attention or are confused.

With online courses, these face-to-face cues are stripped away. If some students don't participate in discussions, how does the instructor know where they stand? Perhaps they don't feel a need to participate or maybe they are so confused they don't know what to ask. Maybe their computer system or communication lines are down. What should an online instructor do about students who don't participate?

Techniques That Work

Most training institutions suggest that classroom instructors occasionally elicit answers and comments by name directly from students who don't tend to participate naturally ("What do you think, Jack?"). Also, there is often a policy for instructors to meet privately with nonparticipating students, to offer encouragement to the timid, or recommend additional learning resources to the perplexed. Fortunately, there are online analogs to both these approaches—directed questions used in Web conferencing and synchronous chat sessions, and one-on-one e-mail communications with inactive students.

Perhaps even more useful in Web-based instruction is the opportunity for frequent assignments that are submitted to the instructor via e-mail or posted on the students' home pages. In some Web-based systems, instructors can even monitor and comment on the activities of individual students during small group collaborative work with virtual whiteboards and conferencing. Unlike a classroom instructor, an online instructor can observe the activities of several student teams. In fact, in properly designed Web-based instruction there is no equivalent to students merely showing up and hiding behind passive facial expressions. It is reasonable to compel student activity as a requirement for the completion of an online course.

Keeping Students Signed On and Interested

- Make the online experience personally valuable.
- Offer perks for sticking with the instruction.
- Create barriers of "guilt" for quitting.
- Be flexible with and attentive to individual students.
- Participating students really want to complete the training.
- Course content must be updated frequently.

Retaining Online Students

The drop-out rate for online students is generally much higher than it is for similar classroom courses. Under some conditions, more than half the students will not complete the course. Typically, you might not even hear from a substantial number of students after they post their initial introductory message: they seem to evaporate in cyberspace.

There are may reasons for this. An online course often takes 20 to 30 times more calendar days to complete than a comparable classroom course and a lot can happen over that period. Online students are often distracted from their course by work and personal activities.

However, students will stay focused on the coursework and persevere if an online course is structured to motivate them to do that. If it isn't, the course will almost certainly face a retention problem. What special actions can an online course manager take to retain students over the long haul? Here are a several suggestions.

Make the Course Especially Valuable

- Assure that the course is relevant, interesting, and as effective as possible, with ways for the participants to customize the course for their own particular needs.

- Provide frequent, personal, and helpful feedback to individual students.

- Require a practical final product that students can show their supervisors. Display some of these products on the course's Web page.

Provide Incentives for Completion

- Offer a prestigious-sounding certificate for successful completion of the course. Make sure this certification or diploma is something students will value.

● Arrange for participants' names, pictures, and even course progress status to be displayed on Web page.

● Arrange and publicize a lottery drawing for a prize to be awarded to someone who has completed the course.

Make It Embarrassing to Drop Out

● When they register, have all participants "sign" a commitment contract to complete the course. If appropriate, have the participant's supervisor cosign the contract.

● Arrange for peer pressure by forming participants into pairs or teams that will work together through the course.

Eliminate Barriers to Completion

● Contact participants' supervisors and notify them that their subordinates are in the course. If possible, negotiate for release time during working hours for students to work on the course.

● Send personal messages to individual participants—especially "lurkers"— asking specific questions about their situations and progress, and offering help.

● Break the course up into reasonable-sized chunks so that any one part can be completed fairly quickly.

● Help structure student self-discipline by establishing firm deadlines and milestones for progress.

Integrated Systems for Delivering Online Instruction

A training organization operating on a limited budget could probably use its existing Internet or intranet client and server software—perhaps supplemented by a few freeware or shareware packages—to put together a suite of most, if not all, of the Web-based capabilities discussed in this book. The difficulty with this approach is that each separate instructional function—conferencing, chats, collaborative work—would have a different look and feel. In addition, the instructors and the students would first have to learn a variety of software operations before they could even get to the course content.

A good alternative to this patchwork approach is to use an *integrated system* for Web-based instruction. Several vendors have packaged a variety of online distance learning functions into a single integrated software product with a common interface across its capabilities. Of course, such a system is more expensive, but it simplifies operations by using common procedures and icons. This section will address three types of integrated systems for conducting Web-based instruction—the *virtual campus* and two very different versions of *virtual classrooms.*

Virtual Campuses

A virtual campus is a software application that organizes all of the operations of the training enterprise, including the delivery of Web-based instruction. When someone accesses the Web site of the training organization, they see the home page of the virtual campus, of which the Web-based classes are only one element. (See figure 4.1.)

The virtual campus home page often provides links to a number of services offered by the institution. The following services are typical:

Registration for New Students

This is available when the student clicks on the "Student Services" hyperlink button on the home page. Students can view a catalog of courses offered, click on the name of a course to inspect the schedule, description and requirements, and—if they are interested—they can open a registration form that can be completed online and submitted to the training administration office.

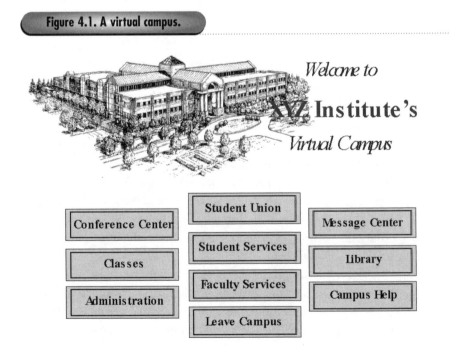

Figure 4.1. A virtual campus.

General E-Mail Services

This service is reached by clicking the "Message Center" button. It provides easy communication to the staff and current students. This service supplements the organization's existing e-mail system by providing directory information about the instructors and students, arranged by course. Clicking on a name in the directory opens the e-mail system and launches an e-mail form with the name of the destination party already embedded in the "To:" block.

Access to an Online Library

Reached by clicking on the "Library" button, this service supplies access to an online catalog of texts, media, and references held by the training organization. The catalog lists the availability of each item and can launch a form to order or reserve materials. The page may also provide links to external library and information services.

Contact With Administrative Offices

When the "Administration" button is clicked, this service offers a menu of information related to training within the organization. This can include policies, procedures, and schedules. A set of frequently asked questions (FAQs) is often provided, along with automatic e-mail access to training managers, so students can ask questions and make comments.

Institute-Wide Web Conferencing

The "Conference Center" button takes students to this service, which offers a Web conferencing capability for general discussions about the training function. (Conferences for specific classes are provided with the *course home page* described in the next section.) Students and faculty can read and participate in a variety of formal debates—How can training be improved? What courses ought to be offered?—and anybody can create a new topical thread for discussion.

Enter a Class

Clicking the "Classes" button opens this service, which provides a menu of current classes that an officially registered student may enter. Clicking on the course names gives direct access to the home pages for specific courses.

Several vendors provide software for a virtual campus. Some, such as *WebCT* (University of British Columbia—http://homebrew1.cs.ubc.ca/Webct), *LearningSpace* (Lotus Institute—http://www.lotus.com), and *TopClass* (WBT Systems—http://www.wbtsystems.com), offer software packages to run on your own server. Others, such as *University Online* (UOL Publishing—http://www.uol.com), will run and maintain the virtual

campus on their server. Prices vary according to the software's capability, the amount of services provided, and the number of students and can range from a few thousand dollars to over $100,000.

Asynchronous Virtual Classroom

A virtual classroom is a software package that integrates the various functions associated with running a course.

Each button link in the virtual classroom opens services for students in the course. (See figure 4.2.) The following services are typical:

Information on Instructors

Clicking the "Your Instructor" button furnishes a biographic sketch of the instructor, often a picture, links to his or her papers and publications, and basic contact information—if not a direct e-mail connection.

Information on Other Students

The "Your Classmates" button offers a roster of the class, contact information of some kind, teams to which students are assigned, perhaps pictures, and sometimes links to students' personal home pages.

Figure 4.2. Home page of an asynchronous Web-based course.

Links to Resources at Other Sites

The "Learning Links" button provides "hot" links to learning resources for the course, which are housed at other Web sites. Each link should be supported with brief annotations describing the size, type, and content of the learning resource.

Access to the Course Materials

Clicking on "Class Materials" opens links to the specific course materials furnished by the instructor. These may include course notes in the form of text and graphics, multimedia presentations, sections of an online textbook, exercises, and tests. Often, this function of a virtual classroom is served by a course outline in a separate frame on the home page: clicking on the name of a course section in the outline opens the appropriate course material.

Submitting Assignments

The "Turn in Assignment" button provides a mechanism for students to send their responses to tests, exercises, projects, or papers to the instructor or to a processing program for assessment or grading. This may be a special e-mail form automatically addressed to the instructor with reference to the assignment and an easy means for uploading, embedding, or attaching the student's work. Another approach is to create a link from the student's home page to the completed assignment, and send a dated e-mail notifying the instructor that the student's assignment has been posted.

Receiving Feedback on Assignments

The "Check Assignment" link permits students to find out the status of the assignments they have submitted. (Were they received by the instructor? Have they been graded yet?). It may also allow them to receive the actual feedback—comments, corrections, or grades.

Participating in Web Conferences

The "Class Conferences" button gives the students access to all the asynchronous Web conferences associated with the course. The instructor may set up a conference on each course module or on specific discussion questions. Through this link, the students can read submissions previously posted to the conference and post new ones of their own. In some packages, students may be given the capability to set up their own discussion thread.

Synchronous Chat Capabilities

The "Discussion Room" button offers links to a listing of active chat sessions related to the course, along with the names of the people who are currently logged on. From here, the student can choose to participate

in a particular session. Although a chat session could be initiated sponta-
neously, these sessions are typically scheduled for a specific time either
by the instructor or by a group of students.

Collaborative Study Group Space

The "Study Groups" link provides a special chat capability for teams of
students assigned by the instructor. The chat operates like the Discussion
Room, except it also has a shared virtual whiteboard. This way student
teams can work together to develop a group project. Typically, this function also allows the student teams to submit shared products to the instructor for grading and feedback.

The vendors who offer virtual campus software also provide asynchronous virtual classroom capabilities in the same packages. A few other
venders offer software packages only for asynchronous virtual classrooms.
These include Virginia Commonwealth University (*Web Course in a Box*—
http://madduck.mmd.vcu.edu/wcb/wcb.html) and SoftArc Inc.
(*FirstClass*—http://www.softarc.com). Several of the software packages
for virtual campuses and virtual classrooms include tools for instructors to
custom plan, design, construct, and revise course materials for their own
Web page formats.

Synchronous Virtual Classroom

Another type of virtual classroom is a specialized software package that
runs simultaneously on both the server and client systems to mimic the
functions of a normal classroom. The instructional session is conducted
synchronously in real time. The screen displayed in figure 4.3 is from one
of these packages called *Brightlight* (from Avalon http://www.atlantis.com/
~avalon).

With this approach, the instructor and the students all log on at a scheduled day and time over a period of weeks, as they would meet in a classroom. Before the live class, the course materials would either have been
downloaded from the training organization's Web site to each student's
hard drive or would have been distributed to each student on a CD-ROM.

During each training session, instructors conduct classes from their
desktops, much as they would from a classroom podium. The individual
students are all seated in front of their computers, either at work or home,
and each has a microphone and a headset or speakers with which to communicate. The instructor uses two capabilities—presentation and interaction—to conduct the classroom session.

Presentation

Much of the session is often taught with a slide show. The large box in
the upper right-hand corner of the screen shown in figure 4.3 usually con-

tains a series of computer graphics controlled by the instructor. It is interesting to note that the slide graphics are not downloaded to the students' PCs as they are presented, but instead have already been stored on each student's computer either from a CD-ROM that the student has inserted earlier, or by an automatic downloading operation that is activated when the student first logs on prior to the class. The instructor merely moves from slide to slide by sending signals over the telephone lines, much as one would use a remote-controlled classroom slide projector: The moment the instructor presses a key, the graphic is changed virtually simultaneously on each student's computer screen.

While the graphic is being displayed, the instructor provides a narration heard over the students' headsets. The instructor can also control overlays that progressively reveal information on the graphic, along with a pointing tool to draw attention to details. In a similar fashion, the instructor can display video clips or demonstrate special software in that large section of the screen while providing recorded or live running commentary. The instructor can even bring up a whiteboard and scribble and talk as he or she would in a classroom. The tree-type diagram in the upper left-hand corner of the screen displays the overall outline of the session, with the current topic highlighted.

Figure 4.3. A virtual classroom.

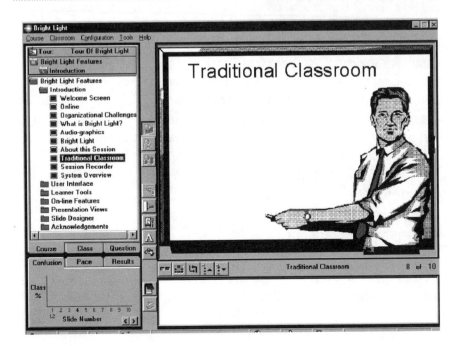

Interaction

In this synchronous virtual classroom, the instructor can interact in much the same way as in a real classroom. He or she can ask questions and direct them to individual students, or wait for a volunteer to answer. The instructor can also delegate *floor control* to any participating student, giving that student control over what everyone hears over their headsets and sees on their computer screens. Of course, the instructor can reclaim floor control whenever he or she wishes.

When the instructor asks a general question, students can raise their hands electronically by clicking on a particular icon: this allows the instructor to see the class roster and to see who is volunteering an answer. The instructor can then give floor control to one of those students to hear their response. Students can also raise their hands electronically at any time to ask the instructor a question.

The software also allows instructors to display multiple-choice questions on the presentation screen, and asks all students to respond by clicking on an appropriate key. The instructor can see the responses of individual students, as well as the responses of the whole class. At any time, students can even click on special icons to indicate that the pace of the class is too fast or too slow or that they are confused. The instructor can see this information in charts in the lower left-hand corner of the screen in figure 4.3.

The students and the instructor can take notes in the section in the lower right-hand corner of the screen, and these notes can be sent back and forth like e-mail, to individuals or to the whole class. The instructor can also bring up a shared whiteboard for collaborative work with the students.

One special feature of the *Brightlight* virtual classroom software is that each session—including all the presentations and interactions—can be recorded by students for playback and review. The instructor can also record the session and make it available to students who miss the class.

Other vendors offer synchronous virtual classroom software with similar capabilities. For example, Interactive Learning International Corporation offers a product called *LearnLink I-Net* (http://www.ilink.com). This product does not currently have the full recording capability of *Brightlight,* but it does include videoconferencing so that students can see a live image of the instructor during the training sessions.

Just Around the Corner

This book was published about nine months after it was written, which is very quick in the publishing field. However, in the field of Web-based

Practical Tips

Integrated Software Packages for Distance Education

● Tools for Developing Interactive Web-Based Courses by the University of Manitoba:http://www.umanitoba.ca/ip/tools/courseware/

● Online Educational Delivery Applications: A Web tool for Comparative Analysis conducted by Dr. Bruce Landon of Douglas College in New Westminster, B.C.: http://www.ctt.bc.ca/landonline/

● Comparing Software for Online Teaching by Murdoch University in Australia: http://cleo.murdoch.edu.au/asu/edtech/webtools/compare.html

instruction, much has probably changed. Because this book focuses on the Web's capabilities for training, the ideas presented here are probably still appropriate. But given the speed of software development, the means for reaching those capabilities may be dramatically different. If I were a betting person, I would wager that several trends have appeared since this book was written:

● More and more people will have access to the networks and systems necessary to conduct Web-based instruction. As a result, the pool of potential students will increase.

● The Web-based instructional systems will be more powerful and faster, with more elaborate "bells and whistles," yet less expensive and easier to use. Consequently, the more sophisticated multimedia techniques will be more common in online courses.

● More extensive use of streaming technologies, better compression techniques, and greater bandwidth capabilities of most organizations' telecommunication systems will significantly reduce the downloading times of course content. This will allow audio and video programming to become more common in online instruction.

● Standard browsers will include elaborate interaction features such as asynchronous conferencing, synchronous chats, and even videoconferencing, so that the more budget-conscious training organizations may not need to acquire specialized Web-based instruction software. Specialized Web-based instruction packages will become even more rich in features than they are now.

● Development of Web-based instruction will begin to become second nature to faculty, as virtually every software page used to produce instructional materials will allow the content to be published in the languages of the Web.

Altogether, it seems that online training soon will be as commonplace as classroom courses. Even the rapidly changing nature of the technology should not pose much of a problem to online trainers because they, perhaps more than anyone, can tap into the power of the Web to stay current.

Glossary

Editor's Note

Confusion continues to surround the term "learning technologies." ASTD has addressed this terminology dilemma by creating definitions for many of the terms associated with the concept of learning technologies. They appear in the following glossary. Terms with an asterisk * in front of the entry title are ASTD-derived terms. All other terms are the author's. For more on terms related to learning technologies, see the November 1997 issue of *Training & Development* magazine.

ASCII: Abbreviation for American Standard Code for Information Interchange—the primary method for encoding text on personal computers. Each character is represented by a seven-digit binary code.

Asynchronous: Communication between two or more people over an extended period of time in which messages are somehow stored so that they can be retrieved at a later time.

*Audio: One-way delivery of live or recorded sound.

Audioconferencing: A form of teleconferencing using telephone technology to communicate with several people at the same time.

Audiographics: A form of teleconferencing involving the simultaneous transmission of telephone and computer (voice and image) signals over telephone lines to one or more distant sites.

Bandwidth: The capacity of a telecommunications channel in terms of how much voice, data, video can be handled at one time.

Bookmark: The name given to an address of a target of a hyperlink. When the bookmark is embedded within a Web page, its name is preceded by the number symbol (#).

Browsers: Software applications that allow Web users to view and navigate through all or part of a hypertext document.

*Cable TV: The transmission of television signals via cable technology.

*CD-ROM (or Digital Video Display): Abbreviation for compact disc-read only memory. A format and system for recording, storing, and retrieving electronic information on a compact disc that is read using an optical drive.

CGI: Abbreviation for *Common Gateway Interface.* A script for processing data written in a Unix-based programming language called *Perl.* It allows form, surveys and other documents to be filled online and the results automatically sent to the Web site's UNIX server.

Chat Mode: Users sending and receiving text or voice messages to and from each other in real time.

Client: Computer system software that occupies a point (or node) on a network and provides functions for users.

Compressed Video: Video images in which the data required for storage and transmission have been reduced by using a compression technique, thereby allowing the images to be sent ever the public telephone network.

Computer-Assisted (or Computer-Based) Instruction: A form of CBT (computer-based training) in which modules of instructional information are presented and student interaction is conducted with the help of computer technology in such a way that learners can proceed at their own pace.

*Computer-Based Training (CBT): A general term used to describe any learning event that uses computers as the primary distribution method; primarily used to refer to text-based, computer-delivered training.

Computer (Web) Conferencing: A form of CBT using computer software that enables people to post or respond to messages on arranged set of topics and subtopics.

Computer-Mediated Communication: A form of CBT that enables communications between or among people.

*Distribution Methods: Means through which information is delivered to learners. Such methods include satellite and cable TV; LAN/WAN networks; computer discs; the Web (the Internet, intranets, and extranets); CD-ROMs; e-mail and voice mail; simulators; audiotapes and videotapes; and telephone.

Desktop Video System: A videoconferencing system in which audio and video images are transferred to the users' desktop computers.

Digital: Information represented in binary form via a series of discrete electronic "zero" and "one" bits that are grouped to represent numbers, letters, or images.

Distance Learning: A system and process that connects learners with remote educational resources.

Domain Name: The verbal address of a Web site (for example, microsoft.com).

Download: The process in which files are transferred from a server to a client.

*Electronic Mail (E-mail): The exchange of messages through computers.

*Electronic Text: The dissemination of text via electronic means.

*Electronic Performance Support Systems (EPSS): An integrated computer application that uses any combination of expert systems, hypertext, embedded animation, or hypermedia to help a user perform a task in real time quickly and with minimal of support from other people.

*Extranet: A collaborative network that uses Internet technology to link organizations with their suppliers, customers, or other organizations that share common goals or information.

FAQs: *Frequently Asked Questions* that are published on a Web page along with standard answers.

File Transfer Protocol (FTP): A technique by which Internet users may send files to and retrieve files from a designated server.

Firewall: A security system that blocks unwanted access to a protected network while giving the protected network access to other networks outside of the firewall.

Frames: The division of a Web page into individual sections, each with its own hypertext reference.

Full-Motion Video: A video transmission format that provides high picture quality comparable to commercial television.

GIF: Abbreviation for Graphic Interchange Format. A compression technique used to save simple graphics.

Gopher: A system by which Internet users can gain access to and view text-based information stored in a particular format.

Graphic Designer: A person skilled in creating and constructing graphic images.

Graphics Tablet: A computer peripheral device that includes a tabletlike drawing surface and a stylus, and which allows images to be transferred to a file while they are being drawn.

*Groupware: An integrated computer application that supports collaborative group efforts through the sharing of calendars for project management and scheduling, collective document preparation, e-mail handling, shared database access, electronic meetings, and other activities.

Home Page: The initial page of a Web site that is typically used to present an overview or table of contents of the site and that often incorporates multimedia images.

HTML: Abbreviation for *Hypertext Markup Language.* The language used to define the appearance of text and images on a computer screen. The standardization of the language allows all computer systems connected to the Internet to display roughly the same screens, regardless of their operating systems.

HTTP: Abbreviation for *Hypertext Transport Protocol.* The Internet protocol that allows Web browsers to retrieve information from servers.

Hyperlink: An element of a Web page that when "clicked" brings a different part of the page or an entirely different page to the computer screen.

Hypertext: The technique by which files are linked electronically so that readers can "click" on a highlighted word, phrase or image and "jump" to another file that may be on the same page or an entirely different Web site.

Image Map: A Web page graphic that has separate, active hyperlinks in different parts of the graphic image.

Instructional Design: A systematic process for assessing instructional needs and goals, defining instructional objectives, selecting instructional methods and media, developing materials to accomplish objectives, and assessing results.

*Instructional Methods: Ways in which information is taught to learners. Such approaches include lectures, literature, games, demonstrations, expert panels, case studies, exercises, group discussion, simulations, and role play.

Instructional Strategy: A plan of instructional activities, methods, and media to achieve instructional goals.

Interactive Forms: A Web page whose entries (boxes in which the user can insert text, boxes with a pull-down menu of selections, and selectable buttons) can be submitted to a server for processing.

*Interactive TV: One-way video combined with two-way audio or another electronic response system.

*Internet: A worldwide network of communication lines that now connects millions of computer users in many kinds of organizations.

Internet Protocol (IP) Address: A lengthy numerical address of a system on the Internet.

Internet Relay Chat (IRC): An Internet resource that enables users to communicate with each other in real-time over the network.

*Intranet: A general term describing any network contained within an organization; used to refer primarily to networks that use Internet technology.

ISDN: Abbreviation for *Integrated Services Digital Network*. A digital telecommunications channel that integrates voice, data, and video and is faster than regular telephone transmissions.

JAVA: A standardized programming language for dynamically creating and processing data "objects" (applets) on the Web.

JPEG: Abbreviation for *Joint Photographic Expert Group*. A compression technique used to store and interpret complex graphics.

*Learning Technologies: The use of electronic technologies to deliver information and facilitate the development of skills and knowledge.

Listserv: An electronic mailing list maintained by a specialized software program; allows subscribers to send messages to a large group of people, all at the same time.

*Local-Area Network (LAN): A network of computers sharing the resources of a single processor or server within a relatively small geographic area.

MIDI: Abbreviation for *Music Instrument Digital Interface.* A standard for representing musical information that defines both hardware and software specifications.

Modem: A communications device for both (1) modulation (converting a digital electronic signal to an analog signal so it can be carried over telephone), and (2) demodulation (converting the analog signal at the receiving end back to a digital format so that the receiving computer can process the signal).

MUD, MOO, MAUD: Stands for, respectively, *Multi-User Domain, MUD Object Oriented, and Multi-Academic User Domain.* Internet-based conferencing techniques that provide many users with a common space in which they can communicate with and interact with a simulated environment.

*Multimedia: A computer application that uses any combination of text, graphics, audio, animation, and full-motion video. Interactive multimedia enables the user to control various aspects of the training such as the sequence of content.

One-Way Video/Two-Way Audio: The transmission of both video and audio signals in one direction, generally from an instructor's site to one or more remote sites, with voice-only transmission in the other direction, usually by telephone.

*Online Help: A computer application that provides online assistance to employees.

Plug-In: Sometimes called a "helper," this is a small software program that is run to present specialized kinds of multimedia formats such as sounds and movies.

PDF: Portable Document Format is a standardized format for transferring whole pages and documents from one computer to another. Unlike HTML, the pages are transferred intact, like photographs, so that they look identical no matter what type of browser is used (the appearance of the pages is browser independent). In order to view the document in a PDF form, the browser must make use of a plug-in helper called an *Adobe Acrobat* reader, which can be downloaded free from Adobe Corporation (www.adobe.com).

*Presentation Methods: The ways in which information is presented to learners. Such methods include electronic text, computer-based training, interactive TV, multimedia, teleconferencing, online help, groupware, virtual reality, audio, video, and electronic performance support systems.

Protocol: A term used in telecommunications to identify a particular method for accessing data over a network (as in FTP and HTTP).

Private Network: A telecommunications network reserved for private use by a single organization.

*Satellite TV: The transmission of television signals via satellite.

*Simulator (or Tactile Gear): A device or system that replicates or imitates a real device or system.

Server: Computer system software, usually requiring a high level of storage and processing capability, that performs specialized operations and provides all computers on a network with access to common information.

Streaming Audio or Video: A transmission process by which sound and motion image files are sent to a client system in an active serial form that allows the audio or video to be presented as soon as it is received without waiting for the entire file to be downloaded.

Synchronous: Communication between two or more people that occurs in real time.

TCP: Abbreviation for *Transmission Control Protocol.* Network software that controls the transmission of data over the Internet and is required for computers to communicate with Web servers.

Telnet: A telecommunications system that allows network users to log in or connect to a remote host computer in order to access information stored there, or to use its software.

*Teleconferencing: The instantaneous exchange of audio, video, or text between two or more or individuals or groups at two or more locations.

Thread: A group of associated postings to a Web conference composed of messages and replies to messages that all relate to a single discussion topic.

URL: Abbreviation for *Uniform Resource Locator.* A string of characters that supplies the Internet address of a resource on the Web along with the protocol by which the resources is accessed (for example, http).

*Video: One-way delivery of live or recorded full-motion pictures.

Videoconferencing: A form of teleconferencing using compressed video technology to transmit two-way video images and sound between two or more sites.

Virtual Campus: A software application that gives students access to an integrated set of interactive capabilities such as mailing lists, Web conferencing, and synchronous chat, useful for conducting a course or program of instruction.

Virtual Classroom: A real-time software application that mimics instructor and student processes found in typical classroom environments, including the presentation of information, the asking of questions, and receiving feedback.

*Virtual Reality (or 3D Modeling): A computer application that provides an interactive, immersive, and three-dimensional learning experience through fully functional, realistic models.

*Voice Mail: An automated, electronic telephone answering system.

VRML: Abbreviation for *Virtual Reality Modeling Language.* A language used to define spaces (or *worlds*) on the Web, which are composed of dynamic 3D graphics.

Webmaster: An individual with primary responsibility for the Web server.

Whiteboard: A software application that allows multiple users to enter content (text, graphics, or markings) into a common page or document.

*Wide-Area Network (WAN): A network of computers sharing the resources of one or more processors or servers over a relatively large geographic area.

*World Wide Web (the Web): All the resources and users on the Internet using the Hypertext Transport Protocol (HTTP), a set of rules for exchanging files (see HTTP above).

References

General Information on Distance Learning

American Center for the Study of Distance Education (ACSDE).
http://www.cde.psu.edu/ACSDE/
An organization that promotes distance education research, study, scholarship, and teaching and serves as a clearinghouse for the dissemination of knowledge about distance education.

American Council on Education (1996). *Distance Learning Evaluation*
Guide. **Washington, DC: ACE Central Services.**
A pamphlet with a checklist of questions to help organizations prepare for reviews and anticipate the type of questions reviewers ask when assessing a distance education program.

American Council on Education (1996). *Guiding Principles for*
Distance Learning in a Learning Society. **Washington, DC: ACE**
Central Services.
http://www.acenet.edu/programs/CALEC/Out_Info_Pubs/Outreach_
info.html#guides
A pamphlet containing definitions and values for five major principles designed to help learners, providers of distance learning, and those responsible for overseeing learning quality.

Caso's Internet University.
http://www.caso.com/inhome.html
Articles, courses, and study resources relating to the art and science of online education.

Distance Education Clearinghouse, **University of Wisconsin–Extension.**
http://www.uwex.edu/disted/home.html
Directory with hyperlinks to many resources related to distance education.

The Distance Education Report.
http://www.distance-educator.com/index.html
A monthly online journal containing practical information for professional educators and trainers.

Franklin, N., M. Yoakam, and R.Warren (1996). *Distance Learning: A Guide to System Planning and Implementation.* **Bloomington, IN: Indiana University.**

A guide dealing primarily with the administrative aspects for planning and managing a distance learning system.

Khan, B.H., editor (1997). *Web-Based Instruction.* **Englewood Cliffs, NJ: Educational Technology Publications.**

A series of articles by numerous university-based authors on a wide variety of topics related to online instruction.

Maricopa Center for Learning and Instruction.
http://www.mcli.dist.maricopa.edu/tl/index.html

A search engine specifically for distance learning resources.

Moore, M.G., and G. Kearsley (1996). *Distance Education: a Systems View.* **Belmont, CA : Wadsworth Publishing Co.**

A comprehensive book that provides the history of distance education, the theoretical foundation for its practice, and the technologies and trends supporting its application, including case histories.

Open University of the United Kingdom, International Centre for Distance Learning.
http://www-icdl.open.ac.uk/

ICDL is a world-class documentation center specializing in collecting and disseminating information on distance education worldwide.

Russell, T.L. (1997). *The "No significant Difference" Phenomenon as Reported in 248 Research Reports, Summaries, and Papers (4th edition),* **Raleigh, NC: North Carolina State University.**

An annotated bibliography of studies reporting the lack of significant differences when comparing distance learning to more traditional instructional methods.

Web Page Design

Arpajian, S., and R. Mullen (1996). *How to Use HTML 3.2.* **Ziff-Davis Press.**

A highly colorful and descriptive guide on using HTML to create Web pages.

The Bandwidth Conservation Society.
http://www.infohiway.com/faster/index.html

Techniques for optimizing Web performance while maintaining an appropriate graphical standard.

Glassdog, design-o-rama.
http://www.digiweb.com/honkzilla/design-o-rama/
Wow! What a site! Click on "design-o-rama" when you get to their home page. Good practical content on page design and an interesting delivery approach.

Lemay, L. (1996) *Teach Yourself Web Publishing with HTML 3.2 in a Week,* **3d edition. Indianapolis, IN: Sams.net Publishing.**
Basic desk reference for preparing HTML code but also includes information designing effective Web pages.

Lynch, P., and S. Horton. *Yale C/AIM Web Style Guide.*
http://info.med.yale.edu/caim/manual/contents.html
A complete guide to design of Web sites, pages, graphics, and so forth. Can be downloaded and printed as a single document.

Morris, M.E.S., and R.J. Hinrichs. *Web Page Design: A Different Multimedia.* **Upper Saddle River, NJ: SunSoft Press, A Prentice Hall title.**
This book is for anyone who designs Web pages, manages their design process, or reviews and approves Web pages. It goes a long way toward explaining what makes an effective page and site—not just cool ones.

David Siegel. *Web Wonk: Tips for Writers and Designers.*
http://www.dsiegel.com/tips/
A wonderful online reference for the *details* on creating effective Web pages including page layout, typography, and graphics.

Sun on the Net: Guide to Web Style. **Sun Micro Systems.**
http://www.sun.com/styleguide/
This is a cookbook for helping people create better Web pages. The guidelines represent the opinions and preferences of a group of people within Sun Micro Systems drawn from their own observations, opinions, and judgments about what makes Web pages better or worse.

WebDeveloper.com.
http://www.webdeveloper.com/
One of the top resources on the Web for daily news, how-to articles, product reviews, and downloads of special interest to Web designers.

Weinman, L. (1996). *Designing Web Graphics: How to Prepare Images and Media for the Web.* **Indianapolis, IN: New Riders Publishing.**
Everything you ever wanted to know about constructing images for the Web. Includes information on differences between formats, backgrounds, typography, and ways of designing for different platforms and browsers.

Web Course Design and Tools

Basic Communications Limited, Internet Resources.
http://www.bcl.net
   Links to sources of information on Chat, FTP, Gopher, HTML, and the Internet.

Centre for Curriculum Transfer and Technology.
http://www.ctt.bc.ca/landonline/
   Descriptions and evaluations of integrated online delivery software.

CyberWeb Software, The Web Developers' Virtual Library.
www.Stars.com
   Links to information on authoring, software, multimedia, HTML, and the Internet.

Mauri Collins, and Zane L. Berge. *The Moderator's Home Page.*
http://star.ucc.nau.edu/~mauri/moderators.html
   This page is a set of resources for moderators and moderators-to-be of online discussion in both academic and nonacademic settings.

B.H. Khan, editor (1997). *Web-Based Instruction.* **Englewood Cliffs, NJ: Educational Technology Publications.**
   This book covers all significant aspects of the design, development, delivery, and evaluation of instruction using Internet's Web.... Provides online sources, cases studies, references, and other forms of information.

The Institute for the Learning Sciences. Engines for Education.
http://www.ils.nwu.edu/~e_for_e/index.html
   An approach to online course design using questioning as the basic strategy. Includes a sample with multimedia.

Southeastern University and College Coalition for Engineering Education. Desktop Video Conferencing Product Survey.
http://www3.ncsu.edu/dox/video/survey.html
   A collection of interesting information related to desktop video-conferencing.

University of Manitoba. *Tools for Developing Interactive Academic Web Courses.*
http://www.umanitoba.ca/ip/tools/courseware/
   Discussion of Web-based instruction and an evaluation of current development tools.

University of Michigan. *CSCW & Groupware.*
http://www.crew.umich.edu/~brinck/cscw.html
 Links to articles on "Computer-Supported Cooperative Work"—the study of how people work together using computer technology. Typical topics include use of e-mail, shared databases and hypertext that includes awareness of the activities of other users, videoconferencing, chat systems, and real-time shared applications, such as collaborative writing or drawing.

David Wooley. *Conferencing on the World Wide Web.*
http://freenet.msp.mn.us/~drwool/Webconf.html#commercial
 Links to and descriptions of many Web conferencing software programs.

Ziff-Davis (ZDNet) *The Internet Collaboration Comes of Age.* **(Part of the** *Whole Web Catalog***).**
http://www.zdnet.com/products/internetuser.html
 References, articles, and reviews of collaboration tools that can be used with distance learning.

Sample Courses

Centre for Computer Information Systems and Mathematics.
http://ccism.pc.athabascau.ca/
 Sample online courses in computer science. Note the virtual campus techniques. The menu item "Ride the Wave" provides links to distance learning resources.

Dakota State University. *Web Authoring With FrontPage97.*
http://www.courses.dsu.edu/fp97/
 A free online course for constructing Web pages with Microsoft's FrontPage97. Courses are available for beginners, intermediates, and advanced.

Defense Acquisition University. *Stat Refresher.*
http://www2-cne.gmu.edu/modules/dau/stat/dau2_frm.html
 Fine example of a Web-based course in which the interaction is accomplished by the use of programmed software. Also contains an interesting approach to navigation.

GTE. *Get Smart Customer Tutorial.*
http://www.bbn.com/getsmart/
 An interesting online tutorial that deals with facts about the costs of Web sites, choosing an Internet service provider, and building a Web site.

Carolyn Kotlas. *Learning Over the Internet* **Institute for Academic Technology.**
http://www.iat.unc.edu/guides/irg-38.html

   Courses, curricula, programs, syllabi, and so forth. Links to the growing number of colleges, universities, and other educational institutions that are teaching classes or delivering course materials over the Internet. Links to directories of online courses, syllabi, course materials, and examples of online classes.

Pennsylvania State University. TURF436W *Case Studies in Turf Management.*
http://www.cas.psu.edu/docs/casdept/turf/turf436/turf436.html

   A course built around the use of case studies. Several cases are available. Students are assigned to study groups and given individual and team assignments which are posted to the Web. Extensive use of hyperlinking in the case presentations.

John B. Smith. *WWW Programming.*
http://www.cs.unc.edu/Courses/wwwp-f97/

   An online course taught at the Department of Computer Science at the University of North Carolina in the Fall 1997 semester. Of special interest in this course are the student projects in JAVA posted to the Web site. Check them out.

Spectrum University.
http://www.vu.org/

   An online university offering a wide variety of free courses. An interesting virtual campus model for running courses with hundreds and maybe thousands of students in a class.

University of Newcastle. STAT101 *Introduction to Statistics.*
http://www.fec.newcastle.edu.au/statistics/handbook/stat 101_handbook.html

   Still another approach to teaching statistics. This one has built-in progress checks and links to an online textbook.

University Online. (UOL) *Windows on the Web—Microsoft Explorer Edition.*
http://www.uol.com/website/

   To gain access to this sample course, click on "How it Works" and then select "Demo Course." (Sign their "Guestbook" to gain an ID and Password.) This course makes heavy use of testing to diagnose needs and to check for mastery.

UserActive.
http://www.useractive.com/tutorial/

   Highly interactive courses dealing with HTML coding and Javascript that provide a practice space to do the coding.

About the Author

Jay Alden is director of distance education for the Information Resources Management College of the National Defense University. In this position he defines the distance education strategy for the institution, helps other faculty make the transition to Web-based instruction, and develops and conducts several Web-based courses himself.

In previous positions, he was responsible for executive-level graduate programs in management at the University of Maryland and managed training development and evaluation groups at Xerox Corporation. He was also vice president for research and development for the International Society for Performance Improvement (ISPI) and chair of its Emerging Technology Committee.

Alden has presented sessions or workshops at ISPI and ASTD, as well as conducting other training conferences during the past 12 years. He develops and conducts courses in the use of technology for management at the IRM College and at the University of Maryland. His articles have appeared in numerous journals including *Training & Development* and *HR Horizons.* He also coauthored a chapter on "Case Studies" in the 1996 edition of the *Handbook of Training and Development.*